SpringerBriefs in Business

SpringerBriefs present concise summaries of cutting-edge research and practical applications across a wide spectrum of fields. Featuring compact volumes of 50 to 125 pages, the series covers a range of content from professional to academic. Typical topics might include:

- A timely report of state-of-the art analytical techniques
- A bridge between new research results, as published in journal articles, and a contextual literature review
- A snapshot of a hot or emerging topic
- An in-depth case study or clinical example
- A presentation of core concepts that students must understand in order to make independent contributions

SpringerBriefs in Business showcase emerging theory, empirical research, and practical application in management, finance, entrepreneurship, marketing, operations research, and related fields, from a global author community.

Briefs are characterized by fast, global electronic dissemination, standard publishing contracts, standardized manuscript preparation and formatting guidelines, and expedited production schedules.

Md. Arifur Rahman

Japanese Retail Industry After the Bubble Economy

Development of the 100-yen Shops

Md. Arifur Rahman
Faculty of Business Studies
Bangladesh University of Professionals
Dhaka, Bangladesh

ISSN 2191-5482　　　　　　　ISSN 2191-5490　(electronic)
SpringerBriefs in Business
ISBN 978-981-19-2896-3　　　ISBN 978-981-19-2897-0　(eBook)
https://doi.org/10.1007/978-981-19-2897-0

© The Author(s), under exclusive license to Springer Nature Singapore Pte Ltd. 2022
This work is subject to copyright. All rights are solely and exclusively licensed by the Publisher, whether the whole or part of the material is concerned, specifically the rights of translation, reprinting, reuse of illustrations, recitation, broadcasting, reproduction on microfilms or in any other physical way, and transmission or information storage and retrieval, electronic adaptation, computer software, or by similar or dissimilar methodology now known or hereafter developed.
The use of general descriptive names, registered names, trademarks, service marks, etc. in this publication does not imply, even in the absence of a specific statement, that such names are exempt from the relevant protective laws and regulations and therefore free for general use.
The publisher, the authors, and the editors are safe to assume that the advice and information in this book are believed to be true and accurate at the date of publication. Neither the publisher nor the authors or the editors give a warranty, expressed or implied, with respect to the material contained herein or for any errors or omissions that may have been made. The publisher remains neutral with regard to jurisdictional claims in published maps and institutional affiliations.

This Springer imprint is published by the registered company Springer Nature Singapore Pte Ltd.
The registered company address is: 152 Beach Road, #21-01/04 Gateway East, Singapore 189721, Singapore

Dedicated to
Halima Begum, My Beloved Mother

Acknowledgement

In the name of Allah, the Most Gracious and the Most Merciful.

First and foremost, praise is to ALLAH, the Almighty, the greatest of all, on whom ultimately, we depend for sustenance and guidance. I would like to thank Almighty Allah for giving me the opportunity, determination, and strength to do this study. His continuous grace and mercy are with me throughout my life and ever more during the tenure of this study.

I would like to pay my deep and sincere gratitude to Professor Kazuo Inaba, Ritsumeikan University. In addition to being an excellent supervisor of my Ph.D. study, he is a man of principles and has immense knowledge of research in general and Econometrics in particular. His enlightened mentorship immensely has enthused me to study econometrics, and I have embedded his invaluable guidance in our empirical studies. He introduced me to the new trend of Japanese Retail Economics and how to incorporate data in Japanese version and inadequate previous studies to make a series of our studies one by one successful.

I am also indebted to Associate Professor Natsuka Tokumaru, Ritsumeikan University, who guided me and gave me precious suggestions to start working on the Japanese retail industry. Her knowledge-worthy comments helped to form the foundation of my research work. I am thankful to Professor David Flath to allow me for the discussion about the Japanese retail market and the Japanese distribution system which helped me a lot to think about my research work and drive my study towards making a unique study.

I would also like to express my gratitude to Professor Kiyoto Kurokawa under whom I started Ph.D. journey in Ritsumeikan University and learned the fundamentals of qualitative research. I am also thankful to Professor Muhammad Shariat Ullah of Dhaka University who inspired me to apply for the Ph.D. programme in the Graduate School of Economics of Ritsumeikan University. Also, he guided me throughout my study giving valuable suggestions.

I also appreciate the support of non-teaching staff of the Graduate School of Economics, Ritsumeikan University for all the things that facilitated smooth work of my research. I would also like to pay my regards to the staff of BKC research office for their invaluable support.

I could not have finished this study without the full support of my beloved mother and father, my sisters, and my brothers. Their love, encouragement, and continuous prayer have made me stronger each day on completing this study.

I would like to pay my heartfelt gratitude to the Ministry of Education, Culture, Sports, Science and Technology for giving me an opportunity to pursue my higher studies in Japan with handsome financial support. I would also like to pay my heartfelt gratitude to the authority of Ritsumeikan University for the financial support for my education and living in Japan. I enjoyed my stay in Japan. I am so thankful to my friends at Ritsumeikan University for passing leisure time with badminton, soccer, and fun in first-rate gymnasium of Ritsumeikan in BKC. I am grateful to my Japanese neighbors for their hospitality and prompt advice for any sort of social obstacles staying in Japan.

At last, I would like to pay my heartiest gratitude to my wife Sanji who sacrificed her esteemed 4 years for my study in Japan and inspired me in each step of hurdles of my doctoral study. Her patience and strength to manage family affairs make the journey of my doctoral study facile. It was stubborn for her to take care of three kids in her expatriate life without enough helping hands. I thank my beloved daughters—Aroush and Anayah, and son—Anam, for providing me a cheerful posture at home after day-long study and sometime overnight work towards my thesis finalization.

About This Book

This book investigates the dynamic changes underlying the development of Japanese retail industry over the period of stagnated economy after the bubble economy. As the determinants of Japanese retail stores density, this study explores the effects of exogenous changes after bubble economy and investigates the background of the advent of 100-yen retail stores and strategic approach of 100-yen retail stores during the Japanese stagnated economy. This study also explores the factors which contributed to change the Japanese distribution channel after the 1990s.

Data on Japanese diversified retailing and wholesale industry are used to depict the trend of retail development in Japan. This research adapts the social optimality model by Flath (1990) to examine the determinants of retail chain stores density in Japan.

This study finds that the downward trend of the economy in the 2000s, along with changes in Large-scale Retail Store law, led to the diversification of the Japanese retail market, such that consumers shifted from the most popular department stores to supermarkets and the cheapest retail alternatives. This continuous trend enabled the emergence of 100-yen retail chains in Japan and expanded gradually since the late 1990s.

The empirical results showed that the density of the population has a significant relationship with the number of retail chains, whereas the sizes of stores, sizes of houses, and proliferation of car ownership have an inverse relationship with the number of retail chains. The proliferation of car ownership for shopping has decreased the number of shopping trips of customers by reducing the distance from retail stores to houses in the neighborhood, which has economized their transportation costs.

Contents

1	**Introduction**	1
	1.1 Research Background	1
	1.2 Research Objectives	4
	1.3 Research Significance	4
	1.4 Structure of the Book	5
	References	6
2	**Key Features of Institutional Changes in Japanese Retailing Since the Bubble Period**	9
	2.1 Background of Institutional Changes in Japanese Retailing	9
	2.2 Revision of Retail Store Law: A Turning Point of Modern Retailing in Japan	11
	2.2.1 Retail Regulation Before the 1990s and Its Impact on Japan Retail Industry	12
	2.3 Japanese Stagnated Economy and Structural Changes in Retail Industry	14
	2.4 Socio-economic Structure of Japan and Its Impact on Retail Structure	16
	2.5 Qualitative Changes in Retail Industry (Economics of Retailing and Supply Chain Networking)	18
	References	23
3	**Research Framework**	25
	3.1 100-Yen Retail Chain Shops in Stagnated Economy	25
	3.2 Determinants of Retail Chain Stores' Density	26
	3.2.1 Analytical Models	26
	3.2.2 The Determinants of Density of Retail Chain Stores	31
	3.3 Factors Changes the Structure of Distribution System	34
	References	34

4 Japanese 100-Yen Retail Chains in the Development of the Retail Industry Beginning in the 1990s 37
    4.1 Advent of 100-Yen Retail Chains 37
    4.2 Distinctive Business Strategy of 100-Yen Chain Shops 39
    4.3 Stagnant Economy of Japan and Emergence of 100-Yen Shops 43
    4.4 Diversified Japanese Retailing 44
    4.5 Changes in Retail Law and Emergence of 100-Yen Shops 46
    4.6 Fierce Competition Within 100-Yen Retail Chains 46
    References 51

5 Dollar Stores: A Sense of Small Neighborhoods in the USA 53
    5.1 Background of Dollar Stores 53
    5.2 Size of the Stores 54
    5.3 Location of Stores 54
    5.4 How Dollar Stores Are Competing 56
    5.5 Dollar Stores Create a Sense of Community 56
    5.6 Adverse Effects of Dollar Stores on a Community 59
        5.6.1 Dollar Stores' Employee Management and Exploitation of Workers 59
    References 60

6 Determinants of Retail Chain Diversity in Japan 61
    6.1 Development of Diverse Retail Chain in Japan 61
    6.2 Impact of Socio-Economic Factors on Retail Density 63
        6.2.1 Descriptive Statistics 63
        6.2.2 Empirical Estimation 64
        6.2.3 Effect of Large-Scale Store Law on Retail Chain Density After the 1990s 66
        6.2.4 Discussion 70
    References 71

7 Factors Affecting Changes in Distribution System in Japan 73
    7.1 Background of the Japanese Distribution Structure 73
    7.2 Basic Features of Changes in Distribution Structure 74
    7.3 Factors Affecting Changes in the Wholesale Structure 76
    7.4 Strategic Changes in Distribution Channel 80
    7.5 A New Horizon in the Japanese Distribution System 84
    References 85

8 Summary and Conclusion 87
    8.1 Summary 87
        8.1.1 Emergence of the 100-Yen Retail Chain in the Development of Retail Industry 87
        8.1.2 Determinants of Retail Chain Diversity in Japan 89
        8.1.3 Factors Contributed to Change the Japanese Distribution System 90

		8.1.4 Expansion of Dollar Stores and It's Impact on Small Neighborhood	90
	8.2	Implications for Japanese Retailing	90
	8.3	Implications for Retailing in Bangladesh	92
	8.4	Future Research	93
	Appendix		94
	References		95

Appendix 97

Bibliography 99

Abbreviations

ADB	Asian Development Bank
BD	Bangladesh
DIY	Do-It-Yourself
DSL	Department Store Law
ECR	Efficient consumer response
EDI	Electronic Data Interchange
GDP	Gross Domestic Product
GLS	Generalized Least Square
GMSs	General Merchandise Stores
IO	Input-Output
JP	Japan
ISS	Information Sharing System
IT	Information Technology
JDC	Japanese Distribution Channel
JETRO	Japan External Trade Organization
JR	Japan Railway
LRSLL	Large Retail Store Location Law
LSL	Large Stores Law
LSRs	Large-Scale Retailers
LSRSL	Large-Scale Retail Store Law
METI	Ministry of Economy, Trade and Industry
MIAC	Ministry of Internal Affairs and Communication
MITI	Ministry of International Trade and Industry
MLITT	Ministry of Land, Infrastructure, Transport and Tourism
OLS	Ordinary Least Square
POS	Point of Sales
QR	Quick Response
RDCs	Regional Distribution Centers
REM	Random Effect Model
RFID	Radio Frequency Identification
RIETI	Research Institute of Economy, Trade, and Industry

SCM	Supply Chain Management
SG&A	Selling, General, and Administrative
UDCs	Urban Distribution Centers
WTO	World Trade Organization

List of Figures

Fig. 1.1	No. of major chain stores per 10,000 persons. *Source* Author's calculation based on METI 2004, 2009, and 2016	2
Fig. 2.1	Key features of institutional changes in Japan retail structure	10
Fig. 2.2	Applications for the opening of new Large Scale Retail Stores. *Source* Based on Riethmuller and Chai (1999)	13
Fig. 2.3	The network structure of supply chain between suppliers and manufacturers. *Source* Based on Dong et al. (2004)	20
Fig. 2.4	Average time spent traveling to stores by retail format and by consumer age bracket. *Source* Based on Takei et al. (2006)	22
Fig. 3.1	Research framework. *Source* Author configures the framework based on the discussion in Chap. 4	26
Fig. 3.2	New firms' entry in a market reduce demand of existing firm and firms' exit shift marginal profit (MR) to the remaining firms in the market	29
Fig. 3.3	Transformation of retail structure in Japan	30
Fig. 3.4	Increase in household inventory (storage and reorder) costs persuades increase stores per household	31
Fig. 3.5	Research framework (2). *Source* Author configures the framework based on the discussion in Chap. 2	32
Fig. 4.1	Some basic strategies of 100-yen shops to add value in supply chain. *Sources* Websites of Daiso, CanDo, Seria, and Watts	41
Fig. 4.2	Product supply chain and logistics management system (RFID—"Radio-Frequency Identification" refers). *Sources* Websites of Seria and CanDo	42
Fig. 4.3	Information sharing and managing supply chain. *Source* Based on the annual reports of Seria, CanDo, and Watts, 2013	42
Fig. 4.4	Growth rate of GDP of Japan. *Source* Economic and social research institute, cabinet office, government of Japan	43

Fig. 4.5	Income and consumption expenditure in Japan (monthly average). *Source* Ministry of internal affairs and communications	44
Fig. 4.6	Comparison of department stores and supermarkets in Japan (number of stores and employees). *Source* Research and statistics department, economic and industrial policy Bureau, ministry of economy, trade and industry	45
Fig. 4.7	Annual sales of department stores, supermarkets, convenience stores, and drugstores (trillion yen). *Source* Ministry of economy trade and industry 2013, 2015, 2019	45
Fig. 4.8	Sales per shop of top 100-yen companies. *Source* Author's calculation from websites of Daiso and annual reports of Seria, CanDo, and Watts	47
Fig. 4.9	Trends in sales of top 100-yen companies. *Source* Author's calculation from the websites of Daiso and annual reports of Seria, CanDo, and Watts	48
Fig. 4.10	Trends in Net Income (In this case "net income" refers the residual amount of earnings after all expenses have been deducted from sales.) of top 100-yen companies. *Source* Author's calculation from annual reports of Seria, CanDo, and Watts	48
Fig. 4.11	Profit per sales of top 100-yen companies. *Source* Author's calculation from annual reports of Seria, CanDo, and Watts	49
Fig. 5.1	Dollar Store proximity and competition with food retailers. *Source* Chuck Grigsby et al. (2021), The Geography of Dollar Stores	55
Fig. 5.2	Number of stores and number of employees. *Source* Dollar General and Dollar Tree	56
Fig. 5.3	Dollar Stores' strategies and the consequences to the community. *Source* Dollar General and Dollar Tree and literature from previous studies	57
Fig. 5.4	Net sales and annual revenue. *Source* Dollar Tree and Dollar General	58
Fig. 6.1	Trends of department stores in Japan. *Source* Authors' calculation based on METI 2004, 2009, and 2016	69
Fig. 7.1	Multi-tiered distribution system of Japanese wholesale. *Source* Based on Ito and Maruyama (1990)	75
Fig. 7.2	Growth of wholesale distribution. *Source* Author figures out from the data of Ministry of Economy, Trade and Industry	78
Fig. 7.3	Transfiguring Japanese distribution channel at the end of the 1990s	83
Fig. 7.4	New approach of distribution system by seven-eleven (from March 1998). *Source* Adopted from Meyer-Ohle (2003)	84

List of Tables

Table 2.1	Types of retail stores by the revised law in 1979	12
Table 2.2	Total passenger cars for private use in Japan, 1980–2015	17
Table 2.3	Increase in the size of dwellings, 1988–2015	17
Table 3.1	Expected result of variables	33
Table 4.1	A brief description of the top performers	38
Table 4.2	Distinctive product lines of 100-yen chain shops	40
Table 6.1	Summary of statistics	63
Table 6.2	Spearman's correlation coefficient	64
Table 6.3	Results of OLS regression and random effect model (REM)	67
Table 6.4	Results of OLS regression and random effect model (REM)	68
Table 7.1	An overview of Japanese distribution market from 1985 to 2016	76
Table 7.2	An overview of wholesale distribution structure in Japan	77
Table 7.3	An overview of wholesale distribution by type of employees	78
Table 7.4	An overview of retail distribution by type of employees	79
Table 8.1	Value-added ratio of Bangladesh and Japan ($million)	94
Table A.1	Results of fixed effect regression	97
Table A.2	Results of fixed effect regression	97

Chapter 1
Introduction

The Japanese retail structure has been transformed from an abundance of small retail stores, such as family enterprise stores, to chain stores. Japanese retailers, however, have a long and mixed history, nationally and internationally, with a period of expansion in the 1980s followed by a long period of decline and stagnation. 100-yen retail chains are a new phenomenon in the Japanese retail sector, which had been dominated by high-priced department stores and supermarket chains since the 1990s. This chapter includes background of the study, objectives of the study, significance of the study and structure of the book.

1.1 Research Background

Modern retail formats such as supermarkets, hypermarkets, specialty supermarkets, drug stores, discounters and convenience stores have replaced or are gradually replacing traditional small-scale retail formats like family-owned neighborhood grocers, all over the world (Altenburg et al., 2016). In Japan, as in the US and European developed countries, retail diversity is dominated by varieties of retail chains with little churn. But, Japan, a geographically compact country, has more retail stores per person than the United States or than most European countries (Flath, 1990). Previous studies such as Flath (1990), Flath and Nariu (1996), Ito and Maruyama (1990), Larke (1994), Takei et al. (2006) describe and seek to explain the retail diversity in Japan. There was a notable change in retail density in Japan after the 1990s with continuous variations.

The Japanese retail structure has been transformed from an abundance of small retail stores, such as family enterprise stores, to chain stores. There was a notable change in the Japanese retail industry in the 1990s with continuous variation. The commencement of certain techniques, such as self- service, self-choice, and chain store management, during the 1950s was marked as the beginning of the first phase of retail development in Japan. A period of major transformation in the Japanese retail

© The Author(s), under exclusive license to Springer Nature Singapore Pte Ltd. 2022
Md. A. Rahman, *Japanese Retail Industry After the Bubble Economy*,
SpringerBriefs in Business, https://doi.org/10.1007/978-981-19-2897-0_1

industry commenced in the 2000s. In addition to traditional entities, such as department stores, supermarkets, and convenience stores, new retail business forms are emerging, including mega shopping mall developments led by real estate companies, and Japan railway (JR) terminals being turned into centers.

Macroeconomic changes in the mid-1990s, such as yen appreciation, economic recession, and changes in government regulations, have caused the proliferation of supermarkets, hypermarkets, and mega shopping malls. However, increasing populations in large cities, shrinking populations in Japan, variation in the socio-economic structure, and the gradual shift of the retail structure from in-house operation to online delivery have been reducing the numbers of retail stores per 10,000 persons across Japan in recent years. The following figure shows that the number of chain stores per 10,000 persons have been crumpling from 2004 to 2017 (Fig. 1.1).

Social-economic developments have had an impact and continue to change Japanese retail structure. These social-economic structures of Japan have been changing rapidly since World War II. The major social-economic changes in Japan since 1990 were development of a countrywide railway network, gradual expansion of the size of houses, increasing car-ownership, rising consumer expenditure, increasing aged population, shifting people from rural area to densely populated urban areas, technological innovation, legal forms, and decreasing self-employment. Flath and Nariu (1996) argue against the claimed inefficiency of the Japanese distribution system which had frequently appeared in academic and journalistic writing on Japan as well as in US government position papers. Flath (1990) argued against the firmly entrenched notion that Japan had a dualistic economy in which the distribution sector, unlike some other sectors, was economically backwards and riddled with

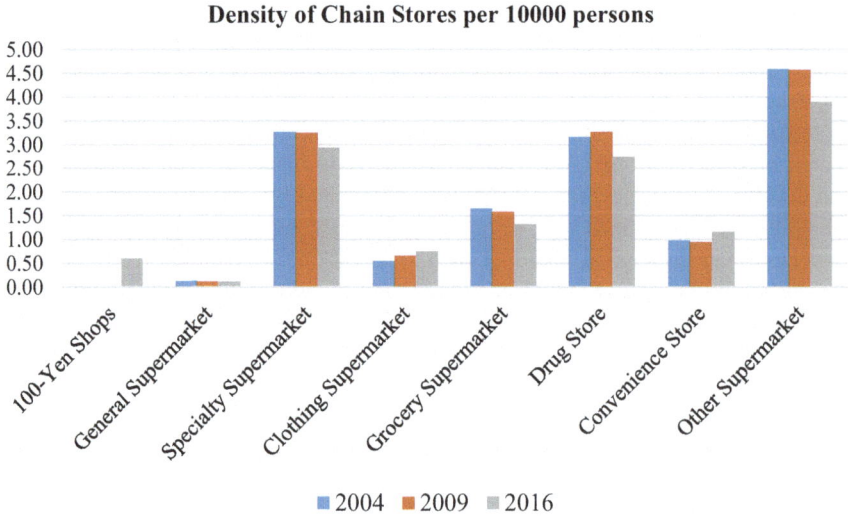

Fig. 1.1 No. of major chain stores per 10,000 persons. *Source* Author's calculation based on METI 2004, 2009, and 2016

anachronistic customs that have a cultural basis rather than an economic basis. In this benighted view, the large number of stores in Japan is a symptom of economically wasteful overemployment in family enterprises, in Lewis' terminology: disguised unemployment. This argument encouraged people in 1990s to establish small stores rather than family enterprise which alleviated the limitations of family enterprise. There is no convincing evidence for any of this.

Flath (1990) argues that retail stores not only distribute consumer goods but also function as a warehouse for people living in the neighborhood. Retailers perform this function because of small Japanese houses. Little space is available for keeping stocks inside the house and people only buy small amounts of daily necessities. Therefore, it has been significant for Japanese retailers to be located close to their clients, in order to make daily shopping convenient. In recent years, in-house storage space has increased since the size of houses have enlarged, and car-ownership has increased rapidly which has eased shopping for Japanese by car instead of on foot. On the other hand, elderly people are assumed to rely on neighborhood stores, because of their lower mobility and their preference for traditional ways of shopping.

Japanese retailers, however, have a long and mixed history, nationally and internationally, with a period of expansion in the 1980s followed by a long period of decline and stagnation. 100-yen retail chains are a new phenomenon in the Japanese retail sector, which had been dominated by high-priced department stores and supermarket chains since the 1990s. 100-yen shops are Japanese-style one-dollar shops, that sell a wide variety of items for 108-yen (8-yen is for tax), is growing rapidly under Japan's low-price retail blocks. The main concept of 100-yen shops is to sell cheap, functional, utilitarian goods that meet the daily needs of consumers. 100-yen retail chains provide their customers with an experience that is enjoyable overall by selling surprisingly high-quality products for their affordable price. This retail chain is constantly working together with designers to develop daily necessary products that capture the hearts of Japanese people and tourists as a souvenir shop.

Shared Research (2018) mentioned that the annual sales of 100-yen shops have grown exponentially since the early 2000s compared to other retail formats. The sales amounted to 700 billion yen in 2017, going from essentially zero in the early 1990s to 500 billion yen by the early 2000s. This rapid growth revealed a niche market that accounted for approximately 1% of total retail sales. Shared Research (2018) and Can Do's (2006) annual report cited that 100-yen retail stores grew in the 1990s against a backdrop of deflation, yen appreciation, and low-cost Chinese labor. After the 1998 Asian currency crisis, the yen's depreciation forced Japan into an industry shakeout that resulted in a four-company oligopoly: Daiso taking first place, Seria in second, Can Do in third, and Watts in fourth place. As each of these companies opened more stores in the 2000s, the rate of growth leveled off as the market neared saturation. Gradually, 100-yen retail chains began to lose their low-price appeal because of growing competition from other retailers. Under these circumstances, 100-yen chain shops expanded their product offerings, introduced products with price points falling outside the standard 100 yen, and moved to develop their businesses overseas.

Flath and Nariu (1996) estimated the effects of social-economic factors on the ubiquity of retail formats among 16 countries including Japan and found that the proliferation of small stores in Japan enables customers to make more frequent shopping trips, maintain low household inventories, and thus economize on scarce living space. The aim of this study is to have better understanding about the structural dynamics of retail industry in Japan. Subsequently, we want to investigate how Japanese retail chain has been changed in the economic recession of Japan after 1990s. This research will also explore the background of the emergence of 100-yen retail chain in Japan. In addition, this study will examine the effect of social-economic factors on the density of retailers.

1.2 Research Objectives

Previous studies on Japanese retailing [e.g., Batzer and Laumer (1989), Flath (1990), Goldman (1991) and the US International Trade Commission (1990)] explored the structure and relative abundance of small stores in Japan which is evident in comparison of the number of stores per thousand inhabitants in Japan with countries like the United States, United Kingdom and Germany. Japanese retailing is undergoing incredible changes—perhaps the widest ranging and most significant change to have occurred in the distribution sector of an advanced industrial country in 1990s (Larke and Causton, 2005). Potjes et al. (1992) cited that economic and marketing in Japanese retailing has increased, because the small scale and the complicated structure of the distribution system is seen as an important impediment to exports to Japan. This study focuses on the dynamic patterns of retail industry in Japan after 1990s which will start describing the economics of retailing, distribution system of Japanese retailing, government regulation of Japanese retailing, and trends of Japanese retailing in economic recession. Therefore, the specific research questions to be answered in this dissertation are as follows:

1.2.1 How have 100-yen shops been expanding?
1.2.2 How has this type of shop been managing a well-equipped supply chain?
1.2.3 How has this type of shop been surviving in the stagnated economy of Japan?
1.2.4 How has the retail sector been changed in Japan after 1990s?
1.2.5 What are the determinants of retail density in Japan?
1.2.6 What are the factors contributed to changes in the Japanese distribution structure after the 1990s.

1.3 Research Significance

Potjes et al. (1992) claimed that Japanese retailing is generally considered to be inefficient, economically backward, outdated and to be riddled with anachronistic customs that have a cultural rather than an economic basis. This opinion is based on the Japan's large number of mom and pop stores relative to the number of stores in modern shop-types such as supermarkets and discount stores. Recent trends show that number of small store and individual enterprises sharply decreased across Japan. A decrease in number of small stores would imply a trend towards increasing the large stores which proves a promising route towards a more efficient Japanese distribution system. In the late 1990s Japan had 11 stores per thousand inhabitants which has been decreased in 10 stores per thousand residents. There are certain key changes in Japanese retail industry after 1950s. Commencement of new technologies, changes in retail law, and access of new retail formats in Japan have made the topic "Japanese retailing" interesting to academic researchers. Large scale retail store law (LSRL) was a key strategic change in the retail industry of Japan in 1992. Apart from this, rapid introduction of the point of sales (POS) system, formation of consumer cooperatives, expanding mail order, flourishing vending machine, and commencement of online sales have opened the new horizons in Japanese retailing. Previous studies on Japanese retailing have yet to uncover the impact of these significant changes in retail dynamics of Japan. This study also cannot treat the overall unrevealed issues of Japanese retailing. So, this research focuses on the structural changes of 100-yen retail chain shops and the determinants of retail density in Japan.

1.4 Structure of the Book

This book is comprised by eight chapters which begins with the introduction of research background, significance of the study and objectives of the research. The subsequent chapters are organized as follows.

Chapter 2 describes relevant literature of the study including Background of Japanese retailing, economics of retailing, distribution system of Japan retail industry, and government regulation on Japanese retailing. This chapter explains about the key economic features of retail market and how did these features affect the retail industry of Japan, about major changes of Retail law after 1990 which have significant impact on proliferation of retail stores in Japan. It also includes explanations about some key socio-economic factors which can determine the density of retail chain stores in Japan.

Chapter 3 elaborates the framework of the study. This study used trend analysis and empirical analysis to investigate the changes in retail structure in Japan. Trend analysis helps us to examine how the retail market is surviving in the stagnated economy of Japan. Also, strategic issues of 100-yen retail chain to maintain well-equipped supply chain are uncovered by trend analysis. Empirical analysis facilitates to reveal the determinants of retail density in Japan.

Chapter 4 investigates the advancement of Japanese retail industry after collapse of the economy in the 1990s. This chapter helps us to investigate the movement of Japanese retailing in the period of economic recession, background of the advent of 100-yen retail chain, and reasons for retail diversification in Japan. This chapter describes about the economic recession and 100-yen retail chain companies' gradual expansion in Japan. Different trend analysis is performed to have a clear view about stagnated economy of Japan and the emergence of 100-yen companies. It also includes brief discussion about the expansion of various retail chain shops with some graphical analysis and trend analysis about sales, sales per shops, net income, and profit per sales of top performers of 100-yen retail chain shops. This chapter unveiled the answers of first three research questions.

Chapter 5 includes the expansion of dollar stores in USA and the impact of dollar stores in small communities of USA. Also, this chapter reveals the secrets of dollar stores to stay competitive in market. In addition, this chapter explores employee management of dollar stores and exploitation of global workforce by dollar stores.

Chapter 5 examines the determinants of retail chain diversity in Japan. This section discusses about how and why Japanese retail market became diversified with numerous types of retail chain. We have discussed here gradual expansion of diversified Japanese retail market in accordance with periodical changes. This section also includes empirical analysis to show the determinants of retail density across Japan. This section also aims to show the impact of socio-economic factors on retail chain density in Japan. This chapter supports to uncover the determinants of retail density in Japan. This chapter uncovered the answers of research questions [1.2.4 and 1.2.5].

Chapter 6 investigates the factors contributing to the changes of Japanese distribution system. This chapter discusses about the basic features of changes in Japanese distribution structure and the factors affecting changes in the wholesale structure. This chapter also explains about the major strategic changes in the Japanese distribution channel after the 1990s. It includes the discussion about new trends of retail formats and distribution structure in Japan. This chapter unveiled the answer of research question–1.2.6.

Chapter 7 concludes the thesis with summary of major findings, concluding remarks about retail and wholesale shops of Japan, relevant limitations and scopes for further research.

References

Altenburg, T., Kulke, E., Hampel-Milagrosa, A., Peterskovsky, L., & Reeg, C. (2016). *Making retail modernization in developing countries inclusive: a development policy perspective*. Discussion Paper 2, German Development Institute

Batzer, E., & ad Laumer, H. (1989). *Marketing strategies and distribution channels of foreign companies in Japan*. Boulder, CL: Westview Press.

Flath, D. (1990). Why are there so many retail stores in Japan. *Japan and the World Economy, 2*, 365–386.

Flath, D., & Nariu, T. (1996). Is Japan's retail sector truly distinctive? *Journal of Comparative Economics, 23*(2), 181–191.

Goldman, A. (1991). Japan's distribution system: institutional structure, internal political economy and modernization. *Journal of Retailing, 67*(2), 154–183.

Ito, T., & Maruyama, M. (1990). *Is the Japanese distribution system really inefficient? National Bureau of Economic Research* (Working Paper No. 3306). Massachusetts, Cambridge.

Larke, R. (1994). *Japanese retailing*. London and New York: Routledge.

Larke, R., & Causton, M. (2005). *Japan—a modern retail superpower*. Palgrave Macmillan, (pp. 225–265).

References

Potjes, J.C.A., Carree M.A., & Thurik, A.R. (1992). *Japanese retail stores: Regulation, retailer-client relations and the dual economy* (Report 9245/A). Netherlands, Econometric Institute, Erasmus University Rotterdam

Shared Research. (2018). Shared Research Inc., Seria. https://sharedresearch.jp/en/2782.

Takei, H., Kudo, K., Miyata, T., & Ito, Y. (2006). Adaptive strategies for Japan's retail industry facing a turning point. *Nomura Research Institute, 110*, 1–13.

US International Trade Commission. (1990). *Phase I: Japan's distribution system and options for improving U.S. Access.* Washington, DC: USITC Publication 2291.

Chapter 2
Key Features of Institutional Changes in Japanese Retailing Since the Bubble Period

This study aims to discuss the prime landmarks of institutional changes in Japanese retail structure. To explore the endogenous and exogenous forces behind qualitative changes in Japanese retail structure, this chapter explains about the major changes of retail law from the 1980s to the 1990s which have significant impact on proliferation of retail stores and how did Large Scale Retail Store Law contributed to expand the number of chain stores in Japan. This section includes the explanations about some key socio-economic factors of Japan which contributed to shift Japanese retail structure from small store-dominance to diversified retail chain-dominance at the end of the 1990s. This chapter also states key economic features of Japanese retail market because of institutional changes after the 1990s.

2.1 Background of Institutional Changes in Japanese Retailing

The 1990s is considered as a period of change and uncertainty for the Japanese economy and its players. Low growth rates, shrinking employment and a growing number of bankruptcies characterized a prolonged period of structural change that is still ongoing. Companies were affected by changes in the 1990s such as deregulation, stagnating consumer demand, internationalization and an unstable financial system. Retail companies that proved to be successful during the 1990s possessed all-round strengths and in many ways point to the future of Japanese retailing. Entering foreign retailers in Japanese market such as Toys 'R' Us, emerging domestic newcomers such as Fast Retailing, and growing convenience stores restructured Japanese retail industry. Two factors such as consumer behavior and deregulation were considered as the major forces driving the development of Japanese retailing and entire distribution system during the 1990s. In addition, changes in socio-economic structure and ongoing stagnated economy brought significant qualitative changes in

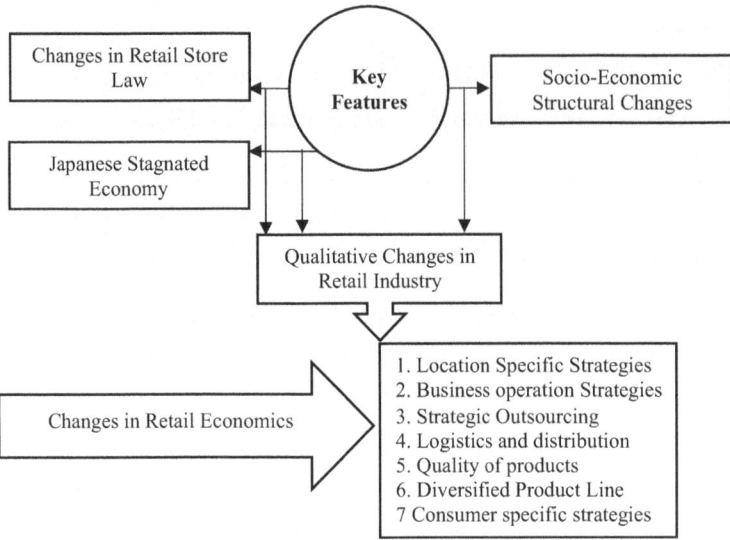

Fig. 2.1 Key features of institutional changes in Japan retail structure

restructuring Japanese retail industry after the 1990s. Figure 2.1 shows the key features of institutional changes in Japanese retail structure after the 1990s.

However, tremendous change has been taking place over the past fifty years in Japanese retailing though some elements of it appeared as traditional and somewhat outdated at the first sight. New retail techniques and retail formats have been introduced continuously. Many innovations in Japanese retailing were borrowed from or inspired by developments in foreign countries and quite a few occurred within Japan (Meyer-Ohle, 2003).

Grier (2001) mentioned that the policies aimed at retail industries have come to change at the end of 1990. For instance, these policies began introducing the competition principle after the 1980s then focused on five important issues: privatizing national enterprises, relaxing trade regulations, restricting competition between large retailers and small retailers, strengthening competition policies, and coping with market failure. This initiative opened the door for foreign investors to participate in the Japanese economy and also motivated local entrepreneurs to concentrate on expanding their businesses internationally. Lottanti (2010) noted some significant changes in the Japanese retail market after the revision of the Large Scale Retail Store Law (LSRL) in the 1990s, which caused an increase in the number of large retailers and a decline in the number of small retailers because the small retailers faced severe competition from large retailers and lost regulatory protection, an imposed restriction that is based on the size of retail stores.

Larke and Causton (2005), who treated Japan as a modern retail superpower, found significant polarization occurring between retailers that offer high-end, branded merchandise and those offering generic, low-price goods, with those in the middle

2.2 Revision of Retail Store Law: A Turning Point of Modern Retailing in Japan

squeezed out of existence. They also mentioned that the Japanese retail market has transformed from manufacturer dominance to retailer dominance after 1990. Consequently, Japanese retail chains were pushed to think about strategic outsourcing and their entire supply chains.

In addition, the development of a low-cost retail chain was the turning point of the Japanese retail sector in the 1990s. Takei et al. (2006) conducted research on the retail market of Japan and found five important turning points in Japanese retailing. The first turning point in the 1900s involved the development of department stores and a rise in the incomes of persons living in urban areas. The second turning point in the 1950s comprised the growth of GMSs (general merchandise stores). At this time, the number of salaried workers and nuclear families, as well as the household incomes of salaried workers, grew. The third turning point in the 1970s promoted shopping centers and convenience stores, against the backdrop of excessive competition among GMSs, decline of small stores, and price-fixing by stores affiliated with electrical manufacturers. The fourth turning point in the 1990s included building complexes, large-scale suburban shopping centers, and rising supermarkets; however, the appeal of shopping centers in rural areas was declining, there was rampant deflation, and the bubble economy was collapsing. The fifth turning point in the 2010s comprised neighborhood shopping centers and online shopping while excess stores and competition between different retailer types appeared and the polarization of incomes and mosaic pattern of consumption expenditure were visible.

In addition, 100-yen chain stores are the only low-price retailers to struggle with GMSs and supermarkets since their birth. Takei et al. (2006) also identified the low-price blocks in Japanese retailing that were considered to be unaccepted by consumers in Japan in the past, unlike in the United States. However, in recent years, new retail formats such as drugstores, 100-yen shops and volume clothing retailers have grown rapidly and have been popularized as low-price blocks to Japanese consumers. Larke and Causton (2005) found Daiso to be the key player in low-price retail block which is still expanding rapidly, and the popularity of its low-price stores makes finding new tenancies and franchisees very easy indeed. Meyer-Ohle (2003) cited that after relaxation of the LSRL in the 1990s, 100-yen shops transfigured to the floor-shop from track-based street shops, and they also started to expand the scope of business in 1995 to 2000 in the biggest cities, such as Tokyo and Osaka.

2.2 Revision of Retail Store Law: A Turning Point of Modern Retailing in Japan

The Large-Scale Retail Store Law emerged as a part of the regulatory landscape in Japan at the end of the 1990s (Riethmuller, 1994; JETRO, 2003; Watanabe, 1994; and Czinkopta & Kotabe, 2000). Under the law, new store openings, changes in operating hours and store expansions had to gain approval from the Ministry of International Trade and Industry (MITI) before they could occur. MITI sought advice from local businesses (including the operators of small shops) before approval was given for the establishment of new stores or for changes in the mode of operation of existing large-scale stores. The reason for this is that the Law was introduced to protect the interests of small and medium sized retailers.

2.2.1 Retail Regulation Before the 1990s and Its Impact on Japan Retail Industry

The regulations on retailing introduced in 1937 to limiting the size of retail shops in Japan. On that time, the first Department Store Law was legislated to protect the small retailers from the expansion of large department stores. The law was abolished in 1947 and it was re-legislated under the same name in 1956 where it was enacted to legalize a special procedure to expand an existing retail business and/or open new stores with an area larger than 1500 m^2. This regulation, however, could not stop the expansion of large stores. This law only confined the number of department stores and did not include other types of retail companies such as supermarket. Also, this law only focused on the expansion of individual retail entity which opened a new strategic window for retail experts to open several business entities (ensuring each individual business outlet not exceeding 1500 m^2) within the same roof.

Therefore, the law was revised again to protect small retailers from severe competition of large retail stores specifically supermarkets. It protected family-operated mom-and-pop stores and existing large stores from new competitors (Riethmuller, 1994). The law reenacted again in 1979 where two types of shops were subject to restrictions (Table 2.1).

Through the 1990s, the government made a number of changes to the Large-Scale Retail Store Law in response to social and economic developments within Japan and the pressure of the United States. The social and economic developments included the increased affluence of the Japanese, a growth in dormitory suburbs outside the major cities and increased westernization. A 1991 change to the regulations altered the definition of what constituted a Category I large store from one with a sales area of 1500 m^2 to one with a sales area of 3000 m^2 while operating hours for large stores were lengthened. Importantly, the 1991 revisions meant that the maximum time for the various applications and approvals to pass through the approval system was set at 12 months (JETRO, 2003).

Table 2.1 Types of retail stores by the revised law in 1979

Type of stores	Description
Type-1 stores	Stores larger than 1500 m^2 (3000 m^2 in large cities): Application to open this type of stores had to be submitted to the Ministry of Trade and Industry (MITI)
Type-2 stores	Stores between 500 and 1 500 m^2: Prefectural offices accepted and approved permission to open this type of stores

A second reform of the Law took place in 1994. Regulations limiting operating hours were relaxed and stores up to 1000 m2 in area were exempted from the approval process. These and other regulatory changes were seen as ushering in lower costs for Japanese retailers and then for consumers. Figure 2.2 shows the number of applications for permission to open new stores lodged with the Ministry of International Trade and Industry. It seems to indicate that at least as far as applications to open new stores were concerned, the change to the Law probably did make a difference. However, the late 1980s and the early part of the 1990s were the years of the bubble economy. It may have been the retailers' expectation that the boom would last forever led at least partly to the large number of applications.

Major Impacts of Large-Scale Retail Store Law:

- The average sales floor area for all retail establishments increased continuously between 2000 and 2015. In 2000, the average Japanese retail establishment (including all stores) had a sales floor space of about 95.2 m^2. As compared to the average sales floor space of 69.1 m^2 in 1991, this corresponds to growth of almost 38%. By 2015, the average sales floor space for Japanese retail establishments had grown further to 116.4 m^2.
- The total sales floor space for retail establishments with 50 or more employees steadily increased between 2000 and 2015.

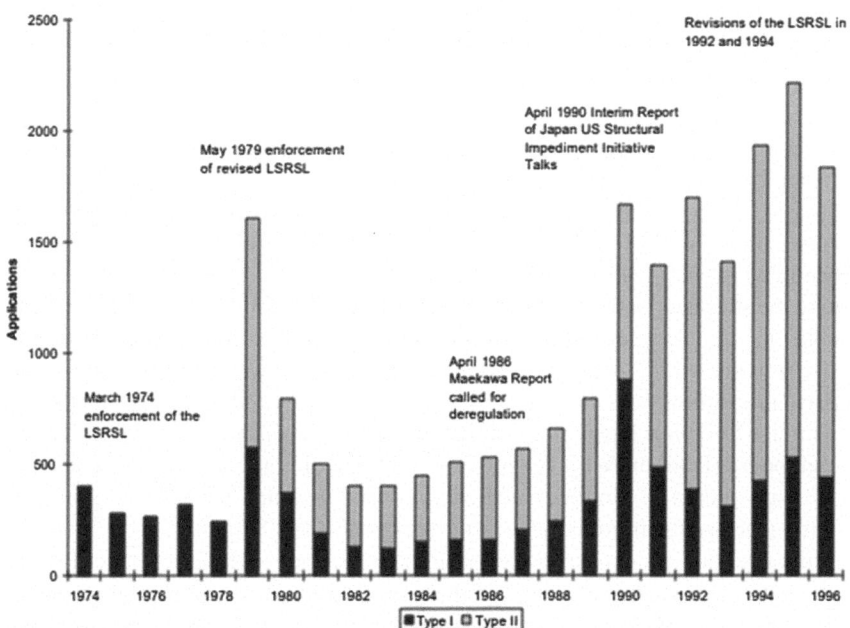

Fig. 2.2 Applications for the opening of new Large Scale Retail Stores. *Source* Based on Riethmuller and Chai (1999)

- The total value of annual sales at retail establishments with 50 or employees exhibited the greatest amount of growth for 1980 (11%), 1990 (8%), 2000 (7%), 2010 (8%), and 2015 (8%).
- The Ministry of Economy, Trade and Industry (METI) provides data on retail establishments with sales floor areas of 500 m^2 or greater for an extended period. Also, retail establishments with sales floor area of between 3,000 m^2 and 6,000 m^2 (Type-1 stores) exhibited the largest increase (42%) at the end of 2001. During the same period, Type-2 stores (6,000 m^2 or larger) also showed two-digit area growth rates: 15% for retail establishments with sales floor area of 6,000 m^2–10,000 m^2.

The remarkable regulatory change at the beginning of the 1990s played a subsidiary role to expand the large-scale retail stores such as supermarkets, drug stores, home centers, specialty supermarkets, and 100-yen retail stores which causes dramatic fall of mom and pop stores in big cities. The effect of large-scale retail store law on the retail chain density is investigated in the 5th chapter where this study explains whether this retail law has any influence to determine the retail chain store density across Japan. Chapter 4 also explains how the retail law contributed to change the retail structure of Japan and expand low cost retail chain such as 100-yen retail chain.

2.3 Japanese Stagnated Economy and Structural Changes in Retail Industry

The period between roughly 1985 and 1990 was a time of unparalleled prosperity in Japan. But it was also a gilded age defined by opulence, corruption, extravagance and waste. When the bubble economy years ended, Japan entered a prolonged slump from which it has yet to fully recover. In the second half of the 1980s, Japan had above-trend growth and very low inflation, and Japanese banks were considered among the strongest in the world.[1] Between 1950 and 1973, the Japanese economy doubled in size every seven years, and it had achieved one of the highest standards of living in the world.[2] Yen appreciation against dollar, lowering bank interest, and massive production were the primary reasons for bubble economy in the 1980s.

Through the 1980s Japanese consumers brought products in large quantities, often at high prices (Dawson & Larke, 2004). Purchasing of household durables, fashion in its many guises of clothes, electrical products, toys and jewelry and spending on gifts increased substantially, year on year in the 1980s (Nikkei, 1989). In this period, large retailers expanded their store networks although the number of small retailers declined slightly. At the beginning of the 1990s the business environment for retailers changed in several ways. First, revelations in 1991 that senior politicians

---

[1] Rameshwar Tandon (2005), The Japanese economy and the way forward, New York: Palgrave Macmillan.

[2] Magnus Blomström, Byron Gangnes and Sumner la Croix edited (2001), Japan's new economy, Oxford: Oxford University Press.

had received financial inducements from a major publishing company created the first widespread anti-corruption moves in Japan since the country achieved economic prosperity (Chowdhury, 1989; Far Eastern Economic Review, 1992).

A second major change was the collapse of the bubble economy that had been based on growing property values through the 1980s when the Japan to USA ratio of land asset values rose from 1.5 to over 4. Third, pressure from the USA to open Japanese markets to imported products, potentially sold by foreign retailers, reached new levels of intensity (Itoh, 1991; MITI, 1990; Punke, 1989; US International Trade Commission, 1990). As a direct consequence of this pressure, substantial amendments were made to the LSRSL in 1991 to make the opening of new stores as lenient as it had ever been in modern Japan. Finally, the Kobe earthquake of 1995 disrupted several sections of the economy, causing a sudden fall in GDP. The general slowdown in the economy, and the trigger effect of this sudden disruption, resulted in unemployment.

Consumer confidence was badly shaken by this combination of factors and not surprisingly failed to recover through the 1990s. Consumers reacted to the changed environment of the 1990s by curtailing their retail spending and slowing their replacement rate for products (Dawson & Larke, 2004). Abegglen (2001) claims that deregulation of retailing was complete by 2000. It is true that the LSRSL was abolished, and replaced with the new Large Retail Store Location Law (LRSLL), and that the new law does not specifically aim to curb the activities of large-format retailers in order to protect small independents, but it is now equally clear that this change was not a form of deregulation, rather a change in store development criteria. By the mid-1990s, retailers, perhaps for the first time in the recent history of Japan, had to compete seriously for customers. But the large firms were ill-equipped for this competition, having achieved little in the way of innovation through the 1980s and having simply built more stores to the same model through the 1990s. This lack of innovation put the retailers in severe price competition in the 2000s where various retail chain stores emerged to approach the changing conditions of consumer behavior. The emergence of chains of 100-Yen shops during the 1990s is illustrative of an innovation response to the change in consumer behavior and spending. Many of these either did not exist in the early 1990s or were very small operations with only a few outlets. Now a days, this low-cost retail formats are increasing in the suburban areas. Also, small superstores, discount stores, convenient stores within the Japan Railway stations, and vending retail machines are increasing gradually.

The above discussion helps author to identify the gap of previous research and following sections are developed to explore the hypothesizes of this study in accordance of revealed research gaps.

The growth of the Japanese economy has been fluctuated from the 1990s to the recent decades which has visible impact on the retail consumption in Japan. This study shows the impact of economic slow growth on the expansion of retail chain and changes in the distribution system of Japan in Chaps. 4 and 6.

2.4 Socio-economic Structure of Japan and Its Impact on Retail Structure

The socio-economic structure of Japan has been changing rapidly since world War II. Since 1970, houses have become larger, car-ownership has increased, consumer expenditure has increased, consumer behavior has become more diversified, population has aged, more people have moved into densely populated areas and self-employment has decreased. These socio-economic developments have had their impact on the Japanese retail structure.

Japan implemented a policy for intensifying production and promoting industry after the Meiji Restoration. This led Japan towards an explosive increase in the production and incomes in the urban areas at the beginning of the 1900s. Because of the development of the railway network on this period, it became much easier for people living in rural areas to travel into the cities to shop and so on. This infrastructural change led to the appearance of a new retail format, namely, department stores. Technological innovations and government regulations restrict the expansion of department stores and emerged "general merchandise stores (GMSs)" as a new retail format on the 1950s. The 1970s experienced various environmental changes in Japan which included an increase in the population of suburban areas, a temporary drop in incomes due to tow occurrences of an oil crisis, fierce competition between GMSs, the decline of small, individual stores, and strengthened regulations imposed on GMSs by the Large-Scale Retail Store Law (LSRSL). Collapse of the bubble economy and deregulation of the LSRSL in the 1990s brought massive changes in the retail industry of Japan and made a fierce competition among various retail formats.

In the 1960s, shopping for convenience goods was performed on foot within a 300 m radius of one's dwelling (Yoshino, 1971). Shopping by car was the exception, in part because the number of private cars per person in Japan was lower than in other nations. During the 1970s, the growth in the number of passenger cars per person in Japan averaged 9% per year (Lothia & Subramaniam, 2000). Growth rates were 16.2% between 1980 and 1985, 23.1% between 1985 and 1990, and 18.8% between 1990 and 1995. After 1995, the growth rate slowed to 7.2% (for the period between 1995 and 2000). Between 2000 and 2004, the figure was a mere 0.3%. Nevertheless, between 1990 and 2010, the number of passenger cars for private use almost doubled (Table 2.2).

It was predicted that with the increase in the number of private passenger cars per person, cars would be used more frequently for shopping trips outside one's local neighborhood. As more households came to rely on cars, small stores might lose much of their inherent advantage over large stores.

From the 1920s to the mid-1950s, the average Japanese household had about five members. By 1970, the average number of people per household decreased to 3.41, reflecting the progressive decline in the birth rate through the 1960s. The size of the average household continued to shrink thereafter, consistent with the increase in nuclear family units of the 1970s. In the 1980s, the average number of members per

2.4 Socio-economic Structure of Japan and Its Impact on Retail Structure

Table 2.2 Total passenger cars for private use in Japan, 1980–2015

Year	Total passenger cars for private use (in 1000 s)	Population (in 1000 s)	Passenger cars for private use per person	Growth in %
1980	21,293	117,060	0.182	
1985	25,595	121,049	0.211	15.9
1990	32,177	123,611	0.260	23.2
1995	38,846	125,570	0.309	18.8
2000	42,108	126,926	0.332	7.4
2004	42,506	127,687	0.333	0.3
2009	43,159	128,031	0.505	51.7
2015	43,805	127,095	0.732	45.0

Source Author's calculation based on the data of Ministry of Land, Infrastructure, Transport and Tourism (MLITT) and Automobile Information Division of Automotive Safety Bureau

Table 2.3 Increase in the size of dwellings, 1988–2015

Year	Total number of dwellings (in 1000 s)	Dwelling rooms per household	Area of floor space per dwelling (m^2)	Increase in %
1988	42,007	4.86	89.29	
1993	45,879	4.85	91.92	3%
1998	50,246	4.79	92.43	1%
2003	53,891	4.77	94.85	3%
2008	57,586	4.67	94.13	-1%
2013	60,629	4.59	94.42	0%

Source Statistics Bureau, Ministry of internal affairs and communications

household continued to decline, while the number of one-person households grew steadily. By 2000, the average household had shrunk to 2.67 members. Of 46.78 million households, private households consisting of one or two persons accounted for 52.7% (Table 2.3).[3]

Larger dwellings accommodating fewer people usually offer more storage space. Therefore, households can maintain a larger stock and need to shop less frequently for daily necessities. This has further eroded the value of close neighborhood shops to Japanese consumers and increased the attractiveness of large stores.

Japanese socio-economic structure has been changed significantly after the Meiji restoration. Chapter 5 examines the effect of socio-economic factors on the density of retail chain stores.

---

[3] See the Statistics Bureau of Japan. According to current projections, this average is expected to keep declining in the years ahead, reaching 2.37 in 2025. With the size of the average household shrinking further, the number of households is expected to continue to increase even after the Japanese population starts to decline. The number of households is projected to peak in 2015 and decrease thereafter.

2.5 Qualitative Changes in Retail Industry (Economics of Retailing and Supply Chain Networking)

Some key strategic issues of retailing can be identified after exploring relevant literature on the economics of retailing by Nystrom (1978), Murry and Schneider (2016), and Carden and Courtemanche (2016). The strategic drivers of retail industry are customer, product, logistics and distribution, business operation, sourcing materials, and location. Also, Johansen and Nilssen (2016) identified some specific requirements for the successful operation of a retail business and the competition centers around all of them. Some of them stressed accessibility to the target consumer, maintaining quality products, selecting convenient locations, managing logistics and inventory, the research and innovation of products, and sales promotion.

Consumer

According to Nystrom (1978), the function of the retail store is to provide its customers with the goods they want—when, where, and how they want them. Conroy et al. (2012) cited that core dollar store consumers, broadly speaking, have lower incomes and self-report lower economic statuses than non-dollar store shoppers do. On the other hand, the Izumiya Research Institute[4] (2007) stressed that Japanese consumers are known to be fastidious shoppers who pay close attention to product quality, product selection, and the best-selling products. However, they are also known for their continued loyalty to the brands they have embraced. Larke and Causton (2005) asserted that a 100-yen retail chain is phenomenally popular with school students and that even adults are happy to buy there, as even if a purchased item breaks immediately, the loss is so small that nobody cares. Takei et al. (2006) identified that 100-yen shops are not very preferable to consumers for foodstuffs and daily necessities, whereas convenient stores and departmental stores are highly preferable to consumers for these two categories of needs.

Wide and Distinct Product Line

Meyer-Ohle (2003) mentioned that Daiso wants to provide its customers with an experience that is entirely enjoyable at the fixed price of only 100 yen. In this quest, the company has come up with an electric toothbrush and hand massage sticks and has also widened its selection of watches to 180 articles. The company regards this philosophy as a key to long-term success with the ongoing change of consumer behavior. Shared Research (2018) pointed out that the company is focusing on product development and aims to expand its customer base as part of its product strategy. Specifically, it plans to add products targeting teenaged women. The company also aims to strengthen its product portfolio management by setting data-based standards for making changes to its product lineup. Yamamoto and Whang (2018) illustrated Daiso's product development process. They found that product ideas might come from customers, employees, or suppliers. Customers typically suggested 100 or more

---

[4] A New Era in Japan's Retailing Market: Deregulation Paves the Way for Inroads by Foreign Groups, Special Report 4. https://ratthapr.files.wordpress.com/2007/10/14-15p.pdf.

new ideas or improvements on a daily basis on Daiso's website, effectively letting Daiso crowd-source new product ideas. Daiso also reviewed each category and rebalanced the product line. A new product idea would then be pushed further and developed into a prototype. The merchandise committee members—the merchandisers, buyers, and product specialists—would get together in each category to review the cost and benefit of each new product and determine what to add and what to drop. Once the product was approved, the product team selected the supplier. Kuchikumi (2015)[5] cited that a wide selection of products, affordable items, quality low-cost products, sourcing products from low-cost manufacturers around the world, and a bulk order of products at one time are the competitive advantages of 100-yen chain shops. 100-yen chain shops are competing to offer the most affordable quality products that can meet daily and seasonal demands.

Quality of Product

Flath (1990) identified that Japan's high density of retail stores sell nondurable goods because Japanese dwellings tend to be small and confined, which makes household storage space limited and costly. Takei et al. (2006) found that unlike supermarkets and drugstores, the consumer ratings of 100-yen shops and convenience stores mostly differ by index item. Although 100-yen shops are rated high for low prices (+1.4) and enjoyable experiences (+0.9), they are rated low for quality (-2.2) and level of service (-1.5). Kuchikumi (2015)[6] pointed out that the concept is not unique to Japan, although dollar shops are highly popular in North America. However, Japanese product lines make 100-yen shops unique both nationally and internationally. The Japanese believe in "new and clean," and they are comfortable with throwing things out after using them. Larke and Causton (2005) mentioned that 100-yen shops are small formats and sell large ranges of products but usually at an even lower quality. However, other formats are used to sell comparatively quality products.

Logistics and distribution

Managing logistics and selecting appropriate distribution channels are the prime factors for retail success. A wide range of previous studies focused on logistics and distribution networking. Dong et al. (2004) developed a supply chain network model with manufacturers, retailers, and consumers. They considered m manufacturers, who are involved in the production of a product, which can then be purchased by n retailers, who, in turn, make the product available to consumers located at o demand markets. They denoted a typical manufacturer by I a typical retailer by j, and a typical demand market by k. They depicted the following supply chain network (Fig. 2.3).

---

[5] The evolution of 100-yen shops and how they've changed people's lives. https://japantoday.com/category/features/kuchikomi/the-evolution-of-100-yen-shops-and-how-theyve-changed-peoples-lives.

[6] The evolution of 100-yen shops and how they have changed people's life. https://japantoday.com/category/features/kuchikomi/the-evolution-of-100-yen-shops-and-how-theyve-changed-peoples-lives.

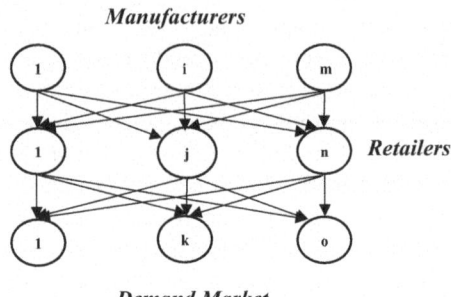

Fig. 2.3 The network structure of supply chain between suppliers and manufacturers. *Source* Based on Dong et al. (2004)

Another research study (Quak & Koster, 2009) focused on urban distribution centers (UDCs). They found that the UDC is a promising concept: the loads of delivery trucks from different carriers are consolidated at a single facility and transferred to new trucks to increase the load factor and to allow for easier time-windowed operations so as to avoid traffic congestion. It is shown from exploring the websites that 100-yen chain shops maintain multi-channel distribution systems and that the top performers have regional distribution centers (RDCs). The RDCs brought economies of scale for these small retailers after the 1990s. Yamamoto and Whang (2018) found that the back-end processing system consisted of four processes: point-of-sale (POS) system use, demand forecasting, inventory management, and distribution logistics. The entire system was developed over a long period, but it was significantly upgraded in 2012. Daiso invested 50 billion yen (approximately $425 million) to establish its eight Japanese RDCs and to renovate the POS technology at all stores in 2014. Daiso continuously reduced its inventory with the POS introduction.[7] The company also introduced radio frequency identification (RFID) e-paper technology to speed up the logistics, and this has integrated three main tasks efficiently: inventory management, manufacturing, and logistics operations.

Strategic Outsourcing

This is another important variable for attaining economies of scale in an organization. Abrahamsson et al. (2003) summarized three types of logistics operations models—decentralized logistics affiliated with top production and marketing, centralized logistics, and direct distribution and logistics platforms—as a resource base for market development. According to Barthelemy (2003), outsourcing is a way for firms to cut costs, improve performance, and focus their limited resources on their core businesses. Larke and Causton (2005) cited that 100-yen chain shops concentrated on China for offshoring manufacturing to attain a low-cost strategy over the retail market. Yamamoto and Whang (2018) mentioned that introducing a highly integrated POS system, demand forecasting, inventory management, and distribution logistics allowed Daiso to automate the whole procurement process. Establishing eight entirely automated Japanese RDCs and the biggest plastic factory in Thailand, as well as the

---

[7] "Core Report," Toyo Keizai Magazine, October 11, 2014.

recent commencement of RFID e-paper technology also contributed to this. For example, the Hiroshima RDC was a 49,587-square-meter center (533,750 square feet) that distributed products to 400 Daiso stores near Hiroshima.[8] Shared Research (2018) mentioned that Seria has a strong collaboration with some reputed suppliers to meet consumers' needs. Seria has 180 dedicated suppliers. Key suppliers include LEC, Inc., Echo Kinzoku Co., Ltd. (unlisted; sells supplies, household sundries, and do-it-yourself items to 100-yen stores), Sun Note Co., Ltd. (unlisted; sells paper products, files, and writing instruments to 100-yen stores), and Kyowa Shiko Co., Ltd. (unlisted; makes and sells paper goods).

Business Operation

Business operation information was found from exploring companies' websites—specifically, top performers among 100-yen chain shops, such as Daiso, Seria, Can Do, Watts, and Lawson. These companies mainly follow two approaches to managing a number of shops across the country and also follow the same strategy for controlling overseas operations. The two main approaches are having company-owned shops and franchising shops. The ownership of shops, cash maintenance, guaranteed fees under a minimum amount in sales, shop maintenance, the product supply chain, product assortment, staff management, a strategic plan, and financial management are the top considerations for both company-owned and franchising shops. The managers of 100-yen chain shops are solely responsible for everything pertaining to company-owned shops. On the other hand, the key functions of a shop, for example—shop maintenance, managing a supply chain of products, product displays in the shop, staff management, an annual strategic plan, and financial control—are performed by the corporate management in franchising shops. Franchisees are responsible only for cash maintenance and guaranteeing a minimum amount in sales per month.

Yamamoto and Whang (2018) identified that Daiso began to develop a new retail model that was less of a treasury hunt model and more of a selected specialty product portfolio to meet customers' latest needs. Examples include Daiso Biz stores, which launched in July 2010 and targeted business districts with selected products. Another example is the Daiso and Aoyama 100-Yen Plaza franchised stores, which launched in June 1999 and used the store spaces of Aoyama Trading Co., Ltd., a fashion retailer in Japan. They also mentioned that Daiso started to expand to markets outside of Japan in 2001. At the beginning, international Daiso stores sold products procured locally, but over time, they migrated to Daiso products to manage the quality and the brand. In terms of this overseas operation, Japanese and non-Japanese stores sold somewhat different products in accordance with the demographic differences of the host countries. Meyer-Ohle (2003) also mentioned that small retailers in Japan, such as 100-yen retail chains, primarily create strong bases in domestic countries to extend their operations overseas.

---

[8] "Strategic Thinking + Logistics Revolution," Nikkan Kogyo Newspaper, April 22, 2015.

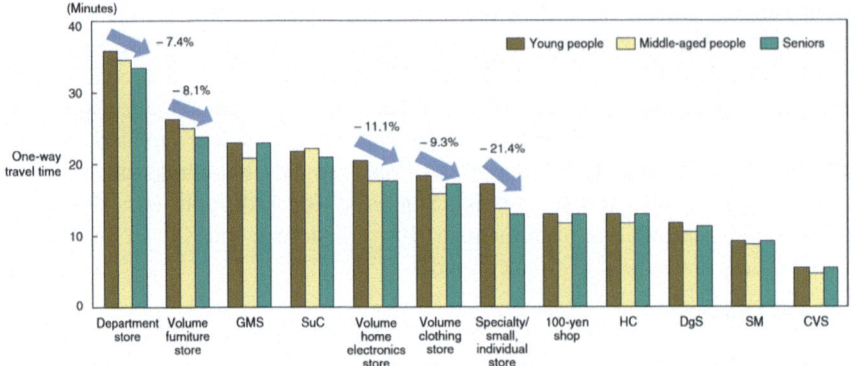

Fig. 2.4 Average time spent traveling to stores by retail format and by consumer age bracket. *Source* Based on Takei et al. (2006)

Location

This is most fundamental to the success of a brick-and-mortar retail business. The use of location intelligence to drive decision-making can be the difference between retail success and failure.[9] Flath (2003) concluded that Japan's relatively high density of retail stores is due to its paucity of private cars, confined household living space, geographic centricity, and super-abundance of trucks. Takei et al. (2006) mentioned that due to the development of the railway network, it became much easier for people living in rural areas to travel into the cities to shop, and this was the first turning point for the expansion of the retail industry in Japan. Also, rapid infrastructural development after the Meiji period encouraged Japanese retailers to find easy-access locations for people. Meyer-Ohle (2003) identified that large food supermarkets and general discount store operators-built stores in locations that were no longer within walking distance of a railway station. Seiyu closed its old branch with its insufficient sales floor and parking near the station, and instead, it opened a new store in a location with good access for car traffic but two kilometers away from the nearest station. Takei et al. (2006) mentioned that compared with younger markets, the senior market showed a relatively low usage frequency in the following four formats: drugstores, GMSs, 100-yen stores, and convenience stores. They also showed a comparison of the time to travel from one's home to a store between seniors and young people, which indicated that seniors need less time than young people do to travel to purchase relatively high-priced goods (Fig 2.4).

---

[9] Critchlow Blog, "Why Location is the Most Important Factor in Retail Success," http://www.critchlow.co.nz/blog/why-location-is-the-most-important-factor-in-retail-success.

References

Abegglen, J. (2001). Prospects for Japan's economy: change and continuity. *Journal of Japanese Trade and Industry, 20*(5), 42–45.

Abrahamsson, M., Niklas, A., & Stahre, F. (2003). Logistics platform for improved flexibility. *International Journal of Logistics: Research and Applications, 6*(3), 85–106.

Barthelemy, J. (2003). The seven deadly sins of outsourcing. *The Academy of Management Executive, 17*(2), 87–98.

Carden, A., & Courtemanche, C. (2016). The evolution and impact of the general merchandise sector. In *Handbook on the economics of retailing and distribution* (pp. 413–432). Edward Elgar Publishing.

Chowdhury, A. (1989). The anatomy of a structural corruption. *Asian Finance, 15*(5), 36–39.

Conroy, P., Muthuraman, K., Kinzler, D., Narula, A., & Nanda, R. (2012). Dollar store strategies for national brands: the evolving dollar channel and implications for CPG companies. Deloitte Research. www.deloitte.com/us/consumerproducts.

Czinkota, M., & Kotabe, M. (2000). Entering the Japanese market—a reassessment of foreign firms' entry and distribution strategies. *Industrial Marketing Management, 29*(6), 483–491.

Dawson, J., & Larke, R. (2004). Japanese retailing through the 1990s: Retailer performance in a decade of slow growth. *British Journal of Management, 15*, 73–94.

Dong, J., Zhang, D., & Nagurney, A. (2004). A supply chain network equilibrium model with random demands. *European Journal of Operation Research, 156*, 194–212.

Far Eastern Economic Review. (1992). Recruit scandals. Far Eastern Economic Review, *155*(13), 22–24.

Flath, D. (1990). Why are there so many retail stores in Japan. *Japan and the World Economy, 2*, 365–386.

Flath, D. (2003). Regulation, distribution efficiency, and retail density (Working Paper 9450). National Bereau of Economic Research, Inc.

Grier, H.J. (2001). Japan's regulation of large retail stores: Political demands versus economic interests. *University of Pennsylvania Journal of International Economic Law, 22*(1), 1–60.

Itoh, M. (1991). *The Japanese distribution system and access to the Japanese market* (pp. 175–190). National Bureau of Economic Research: University of Chicago Press.

JETRO. (2003). A new Era in Japan's retailing market deregulation paves the way for inroads by foreign groups.

Johansen, O.B., & Nilssen, T. (2016). The economics of retailing formats: Competition versus bargaining. *The Journal of Industrial Economics, LXIV*(1), 109–134.

Larke, R., & Causton, M. (2005). *Japan—A modern retail superpower*. Palgrave Macmillan, pp. 225–265.

Lothia, R., & Subramaniam, R. (2000). Structural transformation of the Japanese retail distribution system. *Journal of Business and Industrial Marketing*, 15(5), 323–339.

Lottoanti, M.S. (2010). *The effect of the revised large-scale retail stores law on the Japanese distribution system*. University of Zurich.

Meyer-Ohle, H. (2003). *Innovation and dynamics in japanese retailing: From techniques to formats to systems*. New York, NY: Palgrave Macmillan.

MITI. (1990). Final report of the US-japan structural impediments initiative discussions: A scenario for the new US-Japan Era. Tokyo, MITI Survey Committee

Murry, C., & Schneider, S.D. (2016). The economics of retail markets for new and used cars. In *Handbook on the economics of retailing and distribution* (pp. 343–367). Edward Elgar Publishing.

Nystrom, H. P. (1978). *The economics of retailing*. New York, Third Edition: The Ronald Press Company.

Punke, M.W. (1989). Structural impediments to United States-Japan trade. *Cornell International Law Journal*, 61–62.

Quak, H., & Koster, M. (2009). Delivering goods in urban areas: How to deal with urban policy restrictions and the environment. *Journal Transportation Science, 43*(2), 221–227.

Riethmuller, P. (1994). Recent developments in the Japanese food distribution system. Food Policy, 19(6), 517–532.

Riethmuller, P., & Chai, J. (1999). Japan's large scale retail store law: A cause of concern for food exporters? Paper presented to the International Agribusiness Marketing Association Conference, Florence.

Shared Research. (2018). Shared Research Inc., Seria. https://sharedresearch.jp/en/2782.

Shinbun, NR. (1989). 29th consumer survey: high income consumers. pp. 1–4.

Takei, H., Kudo, K., Miyata, T., & Ito, Y. (2006). Adaptive strategies for Japan's retail industry facing a turning point. Nomura Research Institute, *110*, 1–13.

US International Trade Commission. (1990). Phase I: Japan's distribution system and options for improving U.S. Access. Washington, DC: USITC Publication 2291.

Watanabe, T. (1994). Changes in Japan's public policies toward distribution systems and marketing. In: K. Takeshi (Ed.), *Japanese distribution channels* (pp. 17–34). Binghampton, New York:The Haworth Press.

Yamamoto, K., & Whang, J. (2018). Daiso of Japan: the dollar store. Stanford Graduate School of Business. Case: GS-90.

Yoshino, M. Y. (1971). *The Japanese marketing system: adaptations and innovations*. Cambridge, Massachusetts: The MIT Press.

Chapter 3
Research Framework

This chapter consists of 3 sections according to the purpose to investigate the trends of retail dynamics in Japan to examine the determinants of retail density in Japan, and to explore the factors affecting changes in the wholesale structure of Japan. Each section illustrates the method to explore the research questions in Chaps. 4, 5 and 6. Section 3.1 is based on the process of measuring advancement of 100-yen retail chain in the stagnated economy. Section 3.2 concentrates on the explanation of methods to examine the determinants of retail chain density. Section 3.3 describes the method to investigate factors which change the structure of distribution system.

3.1 100-Yen Retail Chain Shops in Stagnated Economy

To examine the advancement of 100 retail chain shop data are collected for the analysis on the aforesaid research questions; "How 100-yen shops have been expanding, how this type of shops have been managing a well-equipped supply chain, and how this type of shops have been surviving in the stagnated economy of Japan". Relevant data are taken from the current statistics of the Cabinet Office of Japan, the Ministry of Internal Affairs and Communication (MIAC), the Ministry of Economy, Trade and Industry (METI), and the annual and quarterly reports of 100-yen retail companies. Chapter 4 sees the performance of 100-yen shops over past periods under the circumstances of the Japanese and amendment of retail law.

Figure 3.1 shows how 100-yen retail chains have been developing their business under circumstances of the ever-changing external forces like stagnated economy, changes in retail law, emerging new retail formats after the 1990s, since their birth and 100-yen retail chain shops are adopting dynamic strategic issues to cope with the changing atmosphere of Japanese retail industry. This emerging new format always tries to foster its strategy and business model to keep pace with the competition. Wide and distinct product lines, a customer focus, logistics and distribution, business operations, product assortment, product quality, store locations, and strategic

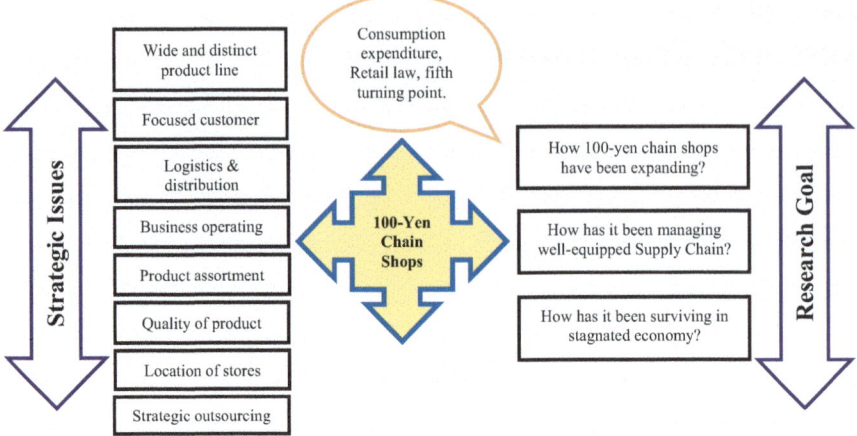

Fig. 3.1 Research framework. *Source* Author configures the framework based on the discussion in Chap. 4

outsourcing are the key strategic concerns of 100-yen shops to remain competitive and manage supply chains efficiently.

Extensive literature is reviewed to examine the key strategic issues of retail businesses, which play a significant role in the survival of low-cost retail chains, such as 100-yen retail chain shops, in the stagnated economy of Japan and in the efficient management of retail supply chain networks. In accordance with Nystrom (1978), these strategic issues are considered to be the economics of retailing. In addition, with the data on household income, household expenditure, and the gross domestic product (GDP) of Japan, evidence of the stagnated economy of Japan is discussed. The data on the Japanese diversified retailing depict the trend of retail development in Japan, and show how Japanese retailing has changed over the period with the changing patterns of the Japanese economy. Moreover, the annual reports on 100-yen retail stores from 1999 to 2018 enable us to understand the development of their top performers. The distinct business strategies of 100-yen retail chains are also considered to justify the research goals.

3.2 Determinants of Retail Chain Stores' Density

3.2.1 Analytical Models

In a distribution system, retailers collect necessary goods from wholesalers or manufacturers and supply it to consumers. On the other hand, consumers perform distribution task by transporting essential commodities from shops to home and storing goods for essential needs. Retail density depends on the economic activities of consumers

3.2 Determinants of Retail Chain Stores' Density

and retailers. There are some well-known models to explain retail density. First, special competition models based on location theory Mills and Lav (1964), Beckmann (1970), Greenhut and Ohta (1973), Hartwick (1973), Stern (1972) assume that price competition can determine the density of stores in an area. They argue that if transportation were costless, firms would have no protection from spatially separated rivals. A firm 1,000 miles away would be just as formidable a competitor as one next door. As a result, space would be of no con sequence. Firms might as well all be located on the head of a pin, perfect competition would prevail. Transport cost gives the spatial firm its monopoly power over customers close to it.

Second, the social optimal model (Flath, 1990)[1] presumes that the density of retail stores minimizes the combined storage and transport costs of households and of the distribution sector. This model logicized that increasing households' cost of storage and reorder due to the changes in institutional regimes bring a rise in the density of retail outlets, which saves household costs by shifting more of the storage and reorder costs onto the retailers. Unlikely, increasing the retailers' costs of storage and reorder due to the changes in institutional regimes bring a fall in the density of retail stores, which saves retailers' inventory costs by changing more of the storage and reorder costs back to the household. Households in greater density areas persuades asymmetrical small increase in the density of retail outlets which causes a smaller number of retail outlets in more densely inhabited provinces. The logic is that increase in number of retail stores per household have less significant effect on the distance to the nearest store for the defined household in densely populated areas compared to sparsely inhabitant areas. That is why marginal benefit of proliferation of retail stores are less significant to the population of greater geographic density. Thus, the extension of retail formats is not so diversified in terms of per household in urban areas compared to rural areas where marginal economic benefits are considered highly because of low income of people in rural areas. It is easy to travel for shopping by walking or light vehicles in rural areas in the neighborhood retailers. On the other hand, due to the unavailability of attractive locations retailers in urban areas are geographically scattered from the inhabitant areas which incline people to use personal cars for shopping trips. The purpose of consumers to economize their household cost shifting their storage and reorder cost on the retailers.

Therefore, the density of retail stores leads to the minimum "social cost of household inventory," which includes consumers' shopping costs and household storage costs together with retailers' reorder costs and storage costs. Flath (1990)[2] argued that the optimization approach for food and other daily necessities is premised on consumers and retailers both having Baumol-type inventory behavior. The density of retail stores leads to the minimum "social cost of product distribution," which is made up of consumers' reorder costs and storage costs. In this context, the optimal level of store density in a given area is[3]:

---

[1] Flath(1990) p. 369.
[2] Flath (1990) p. 368.
[3] Flath (1990) p. 371.

$$n^*/m = (2as/9btm)^{1/2} \tag{3.1}$$

Here, n^* refers the optimal number of retailers, and m denotes the number of households around the perimeter of a circle with circumference 1. We assume that each household buys from the nearest retailer so that each retailer has m/n customers. In addition, a and s denote here customers' shopping (transportation) costs and fixed inventory (storage) cost respectively. Similarly, retailers' reorder cost is b and inventory cost is t.

Third, Nash pricing with free-entry model adopted by Capozza and Order (1978), Salop (1979), Heal (1980), Novshek (1980), and Gabszewicz and Thisse (1986) which represents the pricing choices of retailers as the outcome of a noncooperative game. In accordance with this model the density of retail establishments is the greatest consistent with positive profits. This model argues that when retail pricing is modeled as a Bertrand game with free entry, the equilibrium density of outlets needs not to be socially optimal.

Forth, there were remarkable changes in the retail innovations in Japanese markets from the 1980s to the 2000s where some formats emerge and some formats fade way because of exogenous changes like increasing population in urban areas and increasing number of aging population, development of regional railway and road network, changes in retail law, collapse of bubble economy and stagnated economy followed by the 1990s, emergences of new retail formats, increasing number of car ownership, increasing the size of household and expansion of the size of shop floor. This section presents an explanation for the dynamic innovations of retail markets for consumers' non-durable products after the 1990s. The retail market for consumer non-durable products are mainly divided into dominant firms and competitive fringe. The retail market of Japan was dominated by competitive fringe upto the 1980s where retail law was changed to favor the segment of competitive fringe. The retail segment for non-durable products have long been dominated by the dominant nucleus after the 1990s. The following model conceptualizes this transformation of Japanese retail industry and the impact of this change on the household economy.

Usually, the purchasing cost in the outlets of dominants firms are higher than that of competitive fringe. Before the 1990s, and the establishments of large supermarkets and others chain stores in japan were less numerous and less spread out than those of competitive fringe. It is necessary to keep a defined distance from the residential areas and it is necessary to move greater distances within the stores in terms of dominant nucleus since the size of dominant nucleus outlets has to be larger in accordance of retail store law of 19,991. Shopping trips from household to neighborhood dominant nucleus and long checkout time include transaction cost of consumers, which is worth valued for household economy of Japanese consumers, other than getting products in larger variety than the competitive fringe. The empirical section of this study aims to establish a relationship between household cost and density of retail stores before the 1990s and after the 1990s.

There are n consumers with different purchasing cost and incomes in the retail market. The retail structure in Japan before the 1990s is described as an oligopoly with a competitive fringe. For the long run, the firms of the dominant nucleus (chain

3.2 Determinants of Retail Chain Stores' Density

stores) compete via prices in accordance with Bertrand Model which is not applicable for the small retail stores and individual supermarkets. Generally, chain stores can serve more consumers than they do. Because, the cost increase related to one more customer is almost equal the cost of products sold to the marginal consumer. This study presumes that the segment of competitive fringe of Japanese retail industry before the 1990s had higher marginal cost than those of the dominant nucleus and this trend will, furthermore, increase. It is also assumed that in the long term, offer curve for the competitive fringe is not positively induced because of easy access of new entrants in the fringe segment which is opposite in terms of firms of dominant nucleus. After the 1990s, exogenous changes induced severe competition in dominant nucleus and bring major changes in the Japanese retail structure.

For long run, new entrants in a market increase number of products but reduced the demand of each firms to customers. In addition, profit encourages firms to entry into a new market and entry shifts the demand curves of retailers left. Firms' exit shifts the demand curves of the remaining firms to the right.

Figure 3.2 shows how the density of retailers shifts from competitive fringe to dominant nucleus. The Japanese retail industry was dominated by competitive fringe before the 1990s whereas the density of competitive fringe shifts to the density of firms in a dominant nucleus. This transformation reduced the number of small retailers and large-scale retailers replaced to the small and individual retailers which brought the competitive advantage for larger retailers as the remaining group in the market.

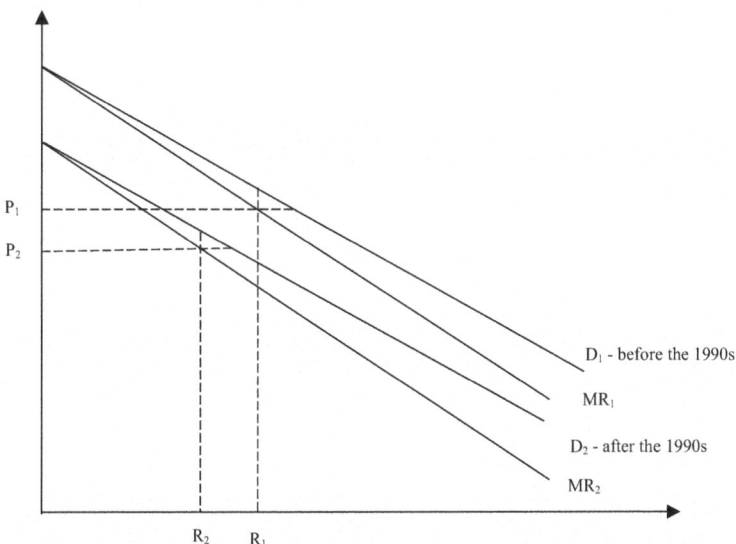

Fig. 3.2 New firms' entry in a market reduce demand of existing firm and firms' exit shift marginal profit (MR) to the remaining firms in the market

Supermarket, convenient stores, specialty supermarkets, and 100-yen retail chain stores emerged as the key players of Japanese dominance nucleus after the 1990s and Japanese competitive fringe like small retail stores confronted fierce competition. Drug stores and supermarkets in JR (Japan Railway) station emerged as alternative retail formats in Japanese dominance nucleus in the 2000s.

Figure 3.3 illustrates that the exogenous changes transformed the retail structure of Japan remarkably from the 1930s to the 2010s and exogenous changes forced remaining firms in the market to bring endogenous changes for staying competitive. The figure shows innovations in Japanese retail market are up warding. The nature of the market changed by the influence of exogenous forces and to meet the contemporary need of consumers in a specific period, innovative retail formats emerged and old formats fade way.

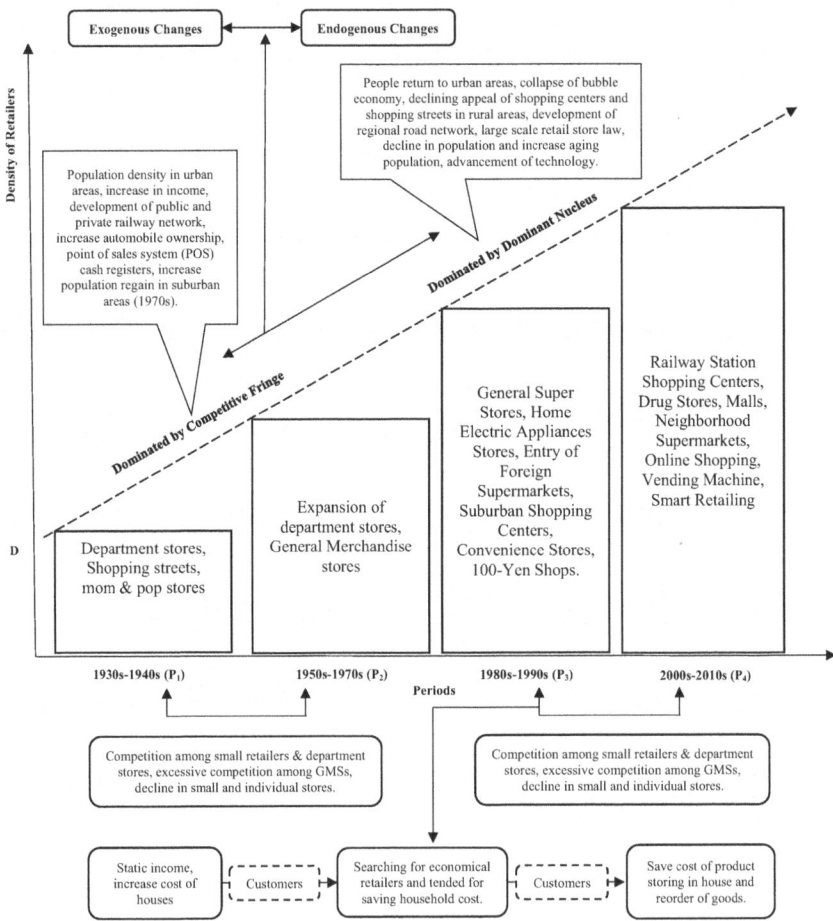

Fig. 3.3 Transformation of retail structure in Japan

3.2 Determinants of Retail Chain Stores' Density

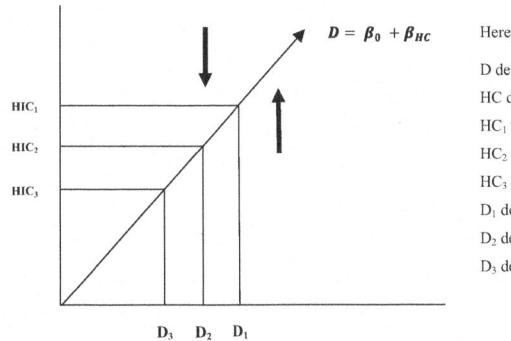

Fig. 3.4 Increase in household inventory (storage and reorder) costs persuades increase stores per household

Figure 3.4 is the continuous effect of household economy on the density of retail store in Japan. Economic recession pursued consumers to economize household cost and to search for cost saving goods. Decrease in individual income derive people to look for economical retailers and to tend for saving household cost. In this regard, cost for storing in house and cost for reorder goods are very important concern to consumer. Figure 3.4 exhibits increasing household cost (HIC) will increase the density of retailers (D) in an inhabitant area. Increase of *HIC* shift the curve of *D* in the right side and the effect of increasing household cost on the density of retailers is upward which shows in the equation "$D = \beta_0 + \beta_{HC}$". Thus, frequent shopping trips in the neighborhood area minimize the storing and reorder cost of customers. Higher price of house spaces induces increasing number of retail chain stores in an inhabitant which makes consumers' shopping trips higher but economize the household inventory cost. The rationality of the model exhibits in the following figure.

The following section introduce the specific model for empirical test of the hypothesis in terms of the logic of the model of this study.

3.2.2 The Determinants of Density of Retail Chain Stores

The discussions of the previous sub-section conceptualize that the variation of retail diversity in the number of stores per household across 47 prefectures of Japan is explained by the proxies of household storage cost and product reorder cost. Equation (3.1) of the previous section is transformed into Eq. (3.2) of log type form as follow:

$$ln(n^*/m) = (1/2)[(ln2/9) + ln(a) + ln(s) - ln(b) - ln(t) - ln(m)] \quad (3.2)$$

Further, the variables in Eq. (3.2) are renamed as those of Eq. (3.3):

$$lnDR_{it} = \beta_0 + \beta_1 lnDPoP_{it} + \beta_2 lnS\_Stores_{it} + \beta_3 lnS\_Houses_{it} + \beta_4 lnCars_{it} + \varepsilon_{it} \tag{3.3}$$

where,

$lnDR_{it} =$	number of retailers per household
$lnDPoP_{it} =$	density of population
$lnS\_Stores_{it} =$	floor sizes of stores
$lnS\_Houses_{it} =$	average size of house
$lnCars_{it} =$	number of cars per household, and
ln	indicates natural log

The subscript of i represents prefecture, and t represents the year of the census of commerce. The variable of ε_{it} denotes the error term. The signs of the coefficients predicted in the theoretical model of this study are $\beta_1 > 0$; $\beta_2 < 0$; $\beta_3 < 0$; and $\beta_4 < 0$.

The followings are two research questions on the determinants of retail density in Japan:

(1) How has the retail sector changed in Japan since the 1990s?
(2) What are the determinants of retail density in Japan?

Chapter 5 examines whether the number of retail stores depends upon the households' costs of storing and transporting goods, the distribution sector's storage and reorder costs, and population density (Fig. 3.5).

Household storage cost and reorder cost are explained by proxy variables such as average size of stores, size of house per person, and motor vehicles per household. The hypotheses of the regression model are that a greater density of household leads to a decrease in the number of retail stores; the increasing sizes of stores decrease the

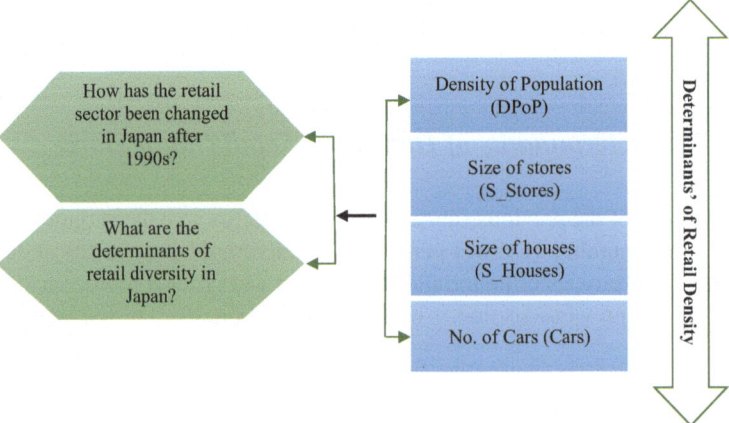

Fig. 3.5 Research framework (2). *Source* Author configures the framework based on the discussion in Chap. 2

3.2 Determinants of Retail Chain Stores' Density

Table 3.1 Expected result of variables

Name of variable	Hypothesis	Expected signs
Density of population (DPoP)	Greater density of household leads to a decrease in the number of retailers	Positive
Size of stores (S_Stores)	Increasing sizes of stores (per square meter) decrease the density of retailers	Negative
Size of houses (S_Houses)	Increases in house sizes induce inhabitants to reduce household inventory costs, which allures retailers to expand geographically	Negative
No. of cars per person (Cars)	In countries where the number of cars per household is more extensive, households have lower costs of transporting goods from stores to dwellings	Negative

density of retail stores; the increase in the house size induces inhabitants to reduce household inventory costs, which allures retailers to expand geographically; and the abundance of cars per household shortens the shipping trips of inhabitants, in addition to reducing the transportation costs. To have these economic effects in household costs, the number of cars per household is increasing in Japan after 2000 though the big cities have car parking shortage due to rising the growth of population (Appendix B). Table 3.1 is the summary of the expected signs of the coefficients.

Previous studies found that retail density in Japan depends on the social benefit of the inhabitants. Flath (1990) constructed an analytical model for explaining the geographical density of retail outlets in an economy. The author explained that retail density in Japan minimizes the consumers' and retailers' combined storage and reorder costs, which is precisely related to cost parameters and to the geographic density of households. This study is the extension of Flath's (1990) study, which used extended data and adapted the OLS model and random effects (GLS) model.

In contrast to Flath (1990), we investigated the impact of the changes in socio-economic variables in a dynamic approach to determine the effects of changes in the number of chain stores on the household inventory costs of inhabitants across Japan from 2000 to 2016. During this period, the living space per person increased almost four times, car ownership almost more than tripled, and a growing number of people were living in the densely populated areas, whereas the number of retail chains per 10,000 persons decreased gradually.

We considered density of population (DPoP), size of stores (S_Stores), size of houses (S_Houses), and number of cars per person (Cars) to be the determinants of the density of retail stores. This study used a total number of retailers (TR_Stores) and diverse formats of chain stores in Japan such, as 100-yen shops, supermarkets (Super_Mkts), other supermarkets (Other_SMkts), drug stores (D_Stores), and convenient stores (C_Stores), as dependent variables because these retail chains are mostly seen in densely inhabited areas, and they sell daily household goods. We adopted log–log specification for variables to minimize the skewness relationship among variables. Data for the number of retailers and store sizes were collected from the census of commerce, conducted by Japan the Ministry of Economy, Trade and Industry (METI). In addition, for population density, house sizes and numbers were collected from the Geospatial Information Authority of Japan, Ministry of Land, Infrastructure, Transport and Tourism (MLITT); the Statistical Survey Department, Statistics Bureau, Ministry of Internal Affairs and Communications; and the Automobile Information Division of Automotive Safety Bureau, respectively. To test the analytical framework, this study used cross-sectional data of 47 prefectures of Japan in 2016, 2009, and 2003. Three years of cross-sectional data were transformed into panel data for more data variation, less collinearity, and more degrees of freedom.

3.3 Factors Changes the Structure of Distribution System

To investigate the factors influenced to change the distribution system of Japan after the 1990s, this research also used data of Japanese wholesale market collected from Ministry of Economy, Trade, and Industry (METI). To show the trend of how distribution structure has been changed over the last two decades, this study used the number of retail and wholesale establishments, growth of sales and number of employees by year. We have also examined how the sales per employee and sales per shops have been changed from 2000 to 2018 which evident the structural changes of distribution system in Japan after the 1990s. The analysis of data and interpretation of descriptive analysis are discussed in the Chap. 6.

References

Beckmann, M. J. (1970). The analysis of spatial diffusion processes. *Papers of Regional Science Association, 25*, 109–117.
Capozza, D. R., & Order, R. V. (1978). A generalized model of spatial competition. *The American Economic Review, 68*(5), 896–908.
Flath, D. (1990). Why are there so many retail stores in Japan. *Japan and the World Economy, 2*, 365–386.
Gabszewicz, J.J., & Thisse, J.-F. (1986). Spatial competition and the location of firms. In JJ. Gabszewicz, J.-F. Thisse, M. Fujita, & U. Schweizer (Eds.), "Location Theory." (pp. 1–71). Chur, Harwood Academic.
Greenhut, M., & Ohta, H. (1973). Spatial configurations and competitive equilibrium. Review of World Economics, Springer; *Kiel Institute for the World Economy, 109*(1), 87–104.
Hartwick, J. M. (1973). Losch's theorem on hexagonal market areas. *Journal of Regional Science, 13*, 213–22.
Heal, G. (1980). Spatial structure in the retail trade: a study in product differentiation with increasing returns. *The Bell Journal of Economics, 11*, 565–583.
Mills, E., & Lav, M. (1964). A model of market areas with free entry. *Journal of Political Economy, 73*, 278–288.
Novshek, W. (1980). Equilibrium in simple spatial or differentiated product models. *Journal of Economic Theory, 22*, 313–326.
Nystrom, H.P. (1978). The economics of retailing, 3rd edn. New York: The Ronald Press Company.

References

Salop, S. C. (1979). Monopolistic competition with outside goods. *The Bell Journal of Economics, 10*, 141–156.

Stern, N.H. (1972). The optimal size of market areas. Journal of Economic Theory, *4*, 154–173.

Chapter 4
Japanese 100-Yen Retail Chains in the Development of the Retail Industry Beginning in the 1990s

100-yen retail chains have emerged as key players in Japanese retailing while the Japanese retail climate in the 1990s has been described overall as rough and highly challenging. 100-yen retail chains gradually started to achieve surprising growth in the market and have become one of prominent retail choices for Japanese consumers. This section describes strategic issues of 100-yen retail chain shops and how has the shops have been surviving with well-equipped supply chain management systems. It provides a clear view of the stagnant economy of Japan and explains how 100-yen retail chains have emerged in the period of recession and how 100-yen retail chains have become key players in the Japanese retail market. This chapter also includes discussion of the expansion of various retail chain stores with graphic analysis of sales and employee trends of those that are dominant in the Japanese market. It gives a trend analysis of sales per shop, net income, and profit per sales of 100-yen retail chain shops.

4.1 Advent of 100-Yen Retail Chains

100-yen shops evolved from truck-based pop-up shops of the 1930s. The predecessors of today's 100-yen shops started by selling stationery, key chains, and other bric-a-brac, with each item priced at 10 sen in the shops' early stages. However, the Japanese retail industry underwent a massive change after the 1990s when the retail law was revised, resulting in the dramatic expansion of the retail sector in Japan and the emergence of low-cost shops like the 100-yen retail chains. Slowly, the idea took hold, and Daiso opened its first 100-yen shop in 1991. The company now runs roughly 4,500 shops nationally and internationally. As seen in Table 4.1, Seria, CanDo, and Watts have 1,506, 1,100, and 920 outlets, respectively. Now, the number of 100-yen chain store companies operating in Japan is more than 15.

Daiso is the pioneer among 100-yen chain shops, selling about 70,000 products, 99% of which are manufactured in company-owned manufacturing plants. More

Table 4.1 A brief description of the top performers

Company Name	Established	Business slogan	Business values	Number of stores		No. of employees (full-time)
				International stores	Domestic Stores	
Daiso	1977	Find surprise and fun	Quality, variety, and uniqueness	1,500 directly managed	3,000 directly managed	721
Seria	1985	Color the days	cleanliness, gratitude, sharing	–	1,506 (51 franchised)	407
CanDo	1993	Something new every day	Quality, surprise, enjoyment, Something new	–	1,100	641
Watts	1995	Always be there	with town, with life, with you	–	920	482

Source Websites of Daiso, Seria, CanDo, and Watts

than 500 products are developed every month. Daiso's core strengths as a company, distinguishing it from competitors, are based on three values: quality, variety, and uniqueness.[1]

Seria, on the other hand, uses the slogan "Color the days" to attract women and places its focus on natural, stylish, and simple products. Seria's main strategy is to attract female customers with its chic and classy products.

The third company, CanDo, is like Daiso: it sells a large variety of lifestyle products and has the unique slogan "Something new every day." CanDo produces its own brand of products[2] called Do! STARS to target young customers. It is also the only 100-yen shop to feature a cute mascot character called Hakken Wando, which is a play on the Japanese word for "discovery", to hint at the deals and products consumers will discover in each store.

The Watts 100-yen shops originally started as two brands, Meets and Silk, which merged to form the Watts brand. The focus of Watts is on stylish home accessories and tidy daily commodities such as kitchenware and stationery.

As an extension of the business model, Lawson created a new business line in 2010 named Lawson 100,[3] which combines a supermarket, a consumer value store, and the 100-yen chain shop. According to Lawson 100's slogan "The best mix", the 24/7 stores sell a variety of items at each 100-yen store (although some items may

---

[1] http://www.daisoglobal.com/products/.

[2] What are the differences between the 100-yen shops? http://100yenshopping.com/differences-100-yen-shops.

[3] Comparing the Big Five 100-yen Shops in Japan. https://guidable.co/shopping-service/comparing-the-five-100yen-shops-in-japan/.

cost more than 100 yen). Lawson 100 handles Yu-Pack (postal package service of Japan Post), allows customers to pay their utility bills, and offers loyalty card services unlike other 100-yen retail chain stores.

However, an in-depth examination of the concepts and theories revolving around Japanese retailing, Japanese retail law, the economics of retailing, and retailers' supply chain networking is needed to understand more about the supply chain process and strategies of 100-yen retail chains to stay competitive in Japan's stagnant economy. The following section aims to explore the aforementioned issues to establish the expected outcomes of this study step by step.

4.2 Distinctive Business Strategy of 100-Yen Chain Shops

(1) Product Line and Product Diversification Strategy

The competitive advantages of 100-yen chain shops consist of the following: a wide selection of products, affordable items, high-quality low-cost products, the ability to source products from low-cost manufacturers worldwide, and the ability to make bulk orders of products. As 100-yen chain shops compete to offer the most affordable quality products that can meet daily and seasonal demands, they are also working to uphold Japanese traditions (Table 4.2).

(2) Specialization of Product Lines

Seasonal Products

Certain seasonal activities are ritualized in the Japanese mindset. Seasonal products specifically include the following: chocolate-making containers and gift wrap for Valentine's Day, wreath and candle decorations for Christmas, and cherry blossom-themed items for the spring. For Valentine's Day and White Day (the day when men who received Valentine's Day chocolates give "return" chocolates to the women and girls who gave them the chocolates), stores display themed wrapping paper, ribbons, stickers, and small bags.

Storage Products

Storage bins and organizers are also popular products at 100-yen stores, because the average Japanese living space is small. This is why 100-yen stores have made it easy to strategize interior storage options in a stylish way. The 100-yen stores offer consumers fashionable draping, multi-colored containers, hanging baskets, racks, and many types of closet and drawer dividers. It is not uncommon for Japanese to measure the odd space in their apartment to make use of unused and awkward spaces, in which they fit small containers, straw baskets filled with supplies, or even a movable mini closet.

Table 4.2 Distinctive product lines of 100-yen chain shops

Company name	No. of products	Types of products	Product strength/specialty	Product specialty
Daiso	70,000	Kitchen goods, cleaning goods, stationery, storage goods, food and drink (incl. wine), cosmetics, toys, gardening products, clothing, pet-related goods; etc	Original items, seasonal and party goods. It is almost like general, DIY, and grocery stores all in one	Daiso develops and produces their own products, including their unique and creative kitchen tool lineup
Seria	20,000	Interior products, kitchen goods, gardening and DIY products	Interior, organizers spacious stores	Focused on female consumer audience, with their chic and classy designed products
CanDo	20,000	Toys, gardening, clothing, interior products, kitchen goods, stationery, storage goods	Food and drinks franchising	Focuses on a large variety of lifestyle products
Watts	18,000	Stationery, storage goods, food and drink, cosmetics, toys, gardening, kitchen goods	Two different brands, "Meets" and "Silk", which merged to form the Watts brand	Targets stylish home accessories and also stylish daily commodities

Source Websites of Daiso, Seria, CanDo, and Watts

Do-It-Yourself (DIY) Products

DIY products are often another distinctive product at 100-yen shops. It is common for Japanese rental spaces to have strict rules regarding the use of nails, painting the walls, and modifying the interiors. To resolve such problems, people go to the 100-yen store for double-sided tape, strong wires that facilitate construction of 100-yen furniture racks, contact paper to adorn walls or cabinets, carpets, and tension rods to create organizational space. Suspension cords, adapters, and electrical cable organizers and connectors can also be purchased at 100-yen stores.

Wide Selection

Many 100-yen stores are essentially one-stop shops, as they offer a wide variety of products, from snacks to kitchenware, basic clothing, office supplies, and even toys. Some 100-yen shops are so big that they can fully occupy a six-floor building. Some 100-yen shops also sell 300-yen or 500-yen products, which makes this retail format more attractive in big cities.

Affordable Items

Most 100-yen shops sell virtually all items for 100 yen, plus the additional consumption tax. That amount is relatively small compared to prices for purchases from department stores, supermarkets, or convenience stores. Cheaper and more expensive items at the 100-yen shops balance each other out, and it is, ultimately, very profitable over a given period.

(3) **Strategies of 100-yen Shops to Add Value in the Supply Chain**

Another competitive strategy of 100-yen chain shops is their uninterrupted supply chain management, which ensures uncluttered product distribution, from production location to shops, through the warehouses of the company. These low-cost chain shops always outsource products from the cheapest production locations in the world and ensure bulk orders to minimize the total cost. Selling mass products through an increasing number of shops is another strategy of 100-yen chain shops, related to the product supply chain. This strategy helps to make these shops competitively profit-oriented in Japan's retail sector (Fig. 4.1).

(4) **Product Supply Chain and Logistics Management System**

For the most part, 100-yen companies maintain supplier relationships in two ways: one is sourcing materials from company-owned manufacturing plants, as Daiso does; another is sourcing products from the cheapest outsourcing plants. Seria, CanDo, and Watts, Daiso's major competitors, rely on both strategies to maintain the supply chain and company inventory. To manage a shorter distribution channel for inventory management, these 100-yen shops maintain direct relationships with manufacturers. Every chain shop has a data management system (POS) that keeps a record of sales data, and this is a shared data management system, between 100-yen chain shops and

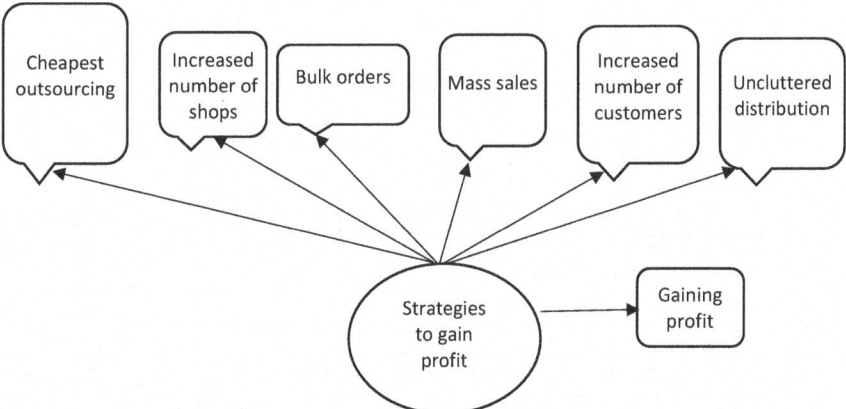

Fig. 4.1 Some basic strategies of 100-yen shops to add value in supply chain. *Sources* Websites of Daiso, CanDo, Seria, and Watts

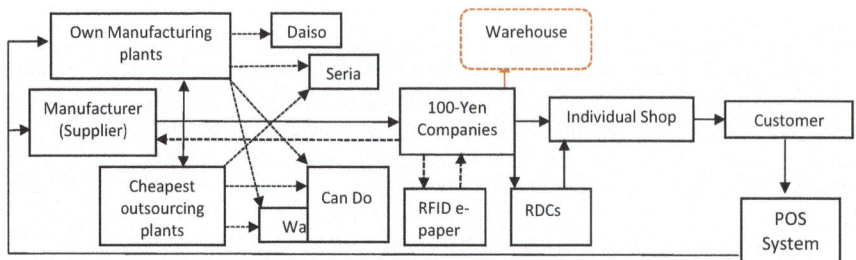

Fig. 4.2 Product supply chain and logistics management system (RFID—"Radio-Frequency Identification" refers). *Sources* Websites of Seria and CanDo

suppliers. Using this system, suppliers and 100-yen shops effectively and efficiently maintain an uninterrupted supply chain of products (Fig. 4.2).

(5) **Information Sharing and Data Management**

Figure 4.3 shows that each 100-yen shop records every transaction, using a POS system. A specialized POS, called the Black Box System, helps 100-yen shops to identify best-selling products and weak-performing products. Instead of a point card system or any other such means, 100-yen shops rely on the Black Box System to identify strong and weak products on their shelves. The data of the POS is automatically synchronized with the corporate information system (IS) at headquarters. Finally, the IS analyzes the accumulated data and produces mathematically filtered data. Consequently, the POS shares all precise data with the designated suppliers, and these data function as support for both corporate management and manufacturers to formulate production and inventory plans (Rahman, 2018). The following figure shows how the POS data work, between individual shops, company headquarters, and suppliers.

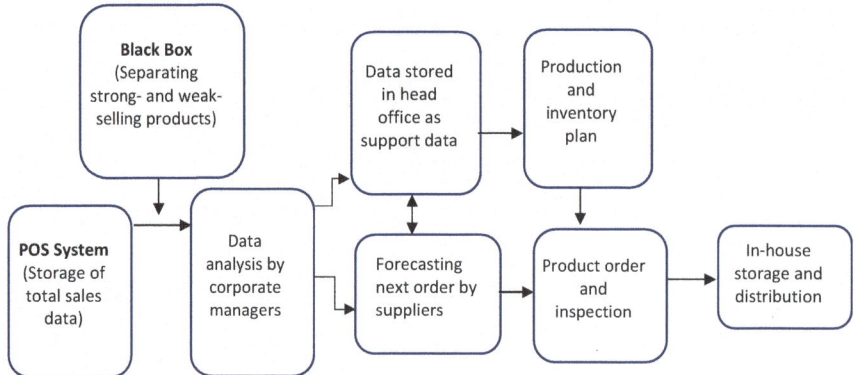

Fig. 4.3 Information sharing and managing supply chain. *Source* Based on the annual reports of Seria, CanDo, and Watts, 2013

4.3 Stagnant Economy of Japan and Emergence of 100-Yen Shops

The GDP growth rate is the most important indicator of the economic health of a country. The GDP growth rate measures how fast the economy of a country is growing. Figure 4.4 shows that Japan experienced a high-growth period for approximately 20 years from the mid-1950s to the early 1970s. The real GDP growth rate frequently exceeded 10% during this period and the highest growth rate was recorded as 13.1% in 1960. Figure 4.4 delineates the general development of Japan's postwar growth rate. The Japanese economy shifted into a period of stable growth in the early 1970s of around 5%, after enjoying the highest growth rate. However, the crash of the bubble in the early 1990s started to cause lower growth rates. In 1998, there was a sharp fall of the growth rate, which is recorded as approximately −2.5%. The real GDP growth rate declined dramatically again in 2009, to −5%, and it has continued to decline, ranging from 1 to 3% currently.

The key driver of GDP growth is personal consumption. Personal consumption expenditure is a measure of national consumer spending that explains how much money people spend on goods and services. Figure 4.5 depicts average monthly income and consumption expenditure of Japanese consumers from 1989 to 2017. It shows that Japanese consumers experienced high income from 1989 to the mid-1990s, peaking at about 600 thousand yen in 1997. Subsequently, the average monthly income started to decrease and, to date, it has remained almost flat. In addition, Fig. 4.5 delineates the consumption trend of Japanese consumers, indicating that consumption expenditure of Japanese consumers gradually increased from 1989 to 1997, then has continued to decline until now, along with the stagnant income level of Japanese consumers.

Fig. 4.4 Growth rate of GDP of Japan. *Source* Economic and social research institute, cabinet office, government of Japan

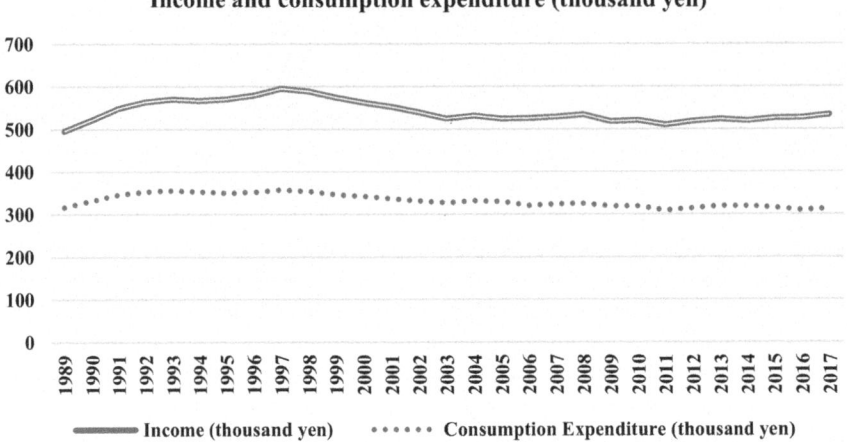

Fig. 4.5 Income and consumption expenditure in Japan (monthly average). *Source* Ministry of internal affairs and communications

Previous studies such as those conducted by Horioka (2006, 2004) found a positive relationship between the stagnant economy and lower consumption. They mentioned that the economic crisis after Japan's bubble economy led to a dramatic decline of consumption in Japan. Heng (2009) and Tsutsui and Mazzotta (2015) found that the major reason for such a dramatic change in consumption was the declining growth rate, from 6.2 to 0.3%, a drop of 5.9% between 1988 and 1993. In addition, Japanese people started to restrict the level of their consumption because of the declining trend in income from the mid-1990s.

4.4 Diversified Japanese Retailing

Retail sales are one of the most important indicators of consumption expenditure. The following figures provide statistical breakdowns of the number of establishments, number of employees, and annual sales of key retail players, which also serve to depict the dynamics of Japanese retailing.

Figure 4.6 provides a comparison between department stores and supermarkets by the number of establishments and number of employees. It shows that both the number of establishments and number of employees of department stores gradually decreased after 2000, whereas the number of establishments of supermarkets started to increase in the same period, although the number of employees remained almost flat in the case of supermarkets. Based on the analysis, it seems that the popularity of department stores among Japanese consumers was decreasing daily, and the acceptability of supermarkets was increasing during the same period; supermarkets are well known as less expensive and as convenient super-shops.

4.4 Diversified Japanese Retailing

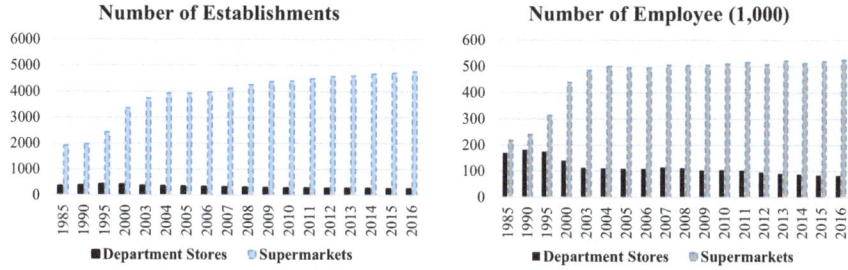

Fig. 4.6 Comparison of department stores and supermarkets in Japan (number of stores and employees). *Source* Research and statistics department, economic and industrial policy Bureau, ministry of economy, trade and industry

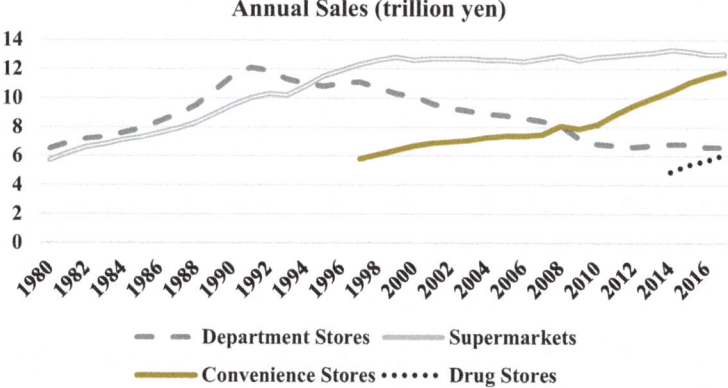

Fig. 4.7 Annual sales of department stores, supermarkets, convenience stores, and drugstores (trillion yen). *Source* Ministry of economy trade and industry 2013, 2015, 2019

Figure 4.7 depicts the important trends of diversified retail sales in Japan. It shows that the sales of department stores gradually increased until 1990, a trend that represents the rising acceptability of department stores among Japanese consumers. But, at the end of the 1990s, department store sales began to fall and continued to do so. Our analysis shows that department store sales fell 6.1% in 2017, the 21st consecutive year of the decline. Sales totaled about 6.1 trillion yen, the lowest since 1980. On the other hand, supermarket sales increased dramatically in the middle of 1990s, and the level of sales has continued to climb over the period, although the growth of sales from one year to another has been very slow since 2000. Nonetheless, it proves that there was a high level of acceptability of supermarkets among Japanese consumers. For convenience stores and drugstores, sales also increased over the period, although the level of sales in both cases remained below that of supermarket sales. In this regard, Nippon.com[4] reported that factors contributing to the decrease in total retail sales include diminished personal consumption due to a string of natural disasters since the summer season, including landslides and floods in western Japan and a major earthquake in Hokkaidō. Stockdill (2011)[5] mentioned 100-yen stores: retail chains of Japan are selling both privately branded and non-brand homewares and living wares and are still growing. It can be concluded, based on the analysis in this section, that Japanese consumers' acceptability of and reliance on the cheapest and most convenient retail formats are increasing; the analysis shows the downturn of the economy and slump in consumption expenditures.

4.5 Changes in Retail Law and Emergence of 100-Yen Shops

Katsumi (2014) indicated that the Large-Scale Retail Law (LSRL) strictly restricted large-scale retailers (LSRs) and protected small and medium-sized retailers from the mid-1970s to the 1990s. The LSRL was amended to ease the opening of new LSRs in 1992. This changing environment in Japanese retailing resulted in the expansion of LSRs, alongside small and medium retailers. Intense competition rose gradually among different formats of retailers, because of the rapid expansion of the retail sector in Japan after 1992. Katsumi (2014) also found consumers were the main beneficiaries of this metamorphosis in retail structure, since it enhanced consumer welfare via a reduction in retail price.

Lottoanti (2010) identified some important changes in Japanese retailing after the revision of the LSRL. Some important drivers were direct sourcing from manufacturers, empowering retailers, initiating a POS system, and relaxing foreign affiliations, which also played a significant role in enabling low-price retailers like the 100-yen shops to survive in the competition. Shared Research (2018) mentioned that 100-yen shops were transformed to competitive retail chains from a truck-based operation after 1990, which is also a reflection of the changing patterns of retail laws.

4.6 Fierce Competition Within 100-Yen Retail Chains

The Japanese retail market is more diversified than the retail markets in other developed countries like Germany or other European countries (Flath and Nariu, 1996). Low-cost retail chains, exemplified by 100-yen shops, have confronted severe competition from other retailers because of new amendments in retail law, the rise and fall

---

[4] https://www.nippon.com/en/japan-data/h00383/japanese-department-store-sales-fall-by-a-third-in-20-years.html, "Japanese department store sales fall by a third in 20 years, February 8, 2019.

[5] Robert Stockdill (2011), "The changing landscape of Japanese retailing", https://www.insideretail.com.au/news/the-changing-landscape-of-japanese-retailing-201104.

4.6 Fierce Competition Within 100-Yen Retail Chains

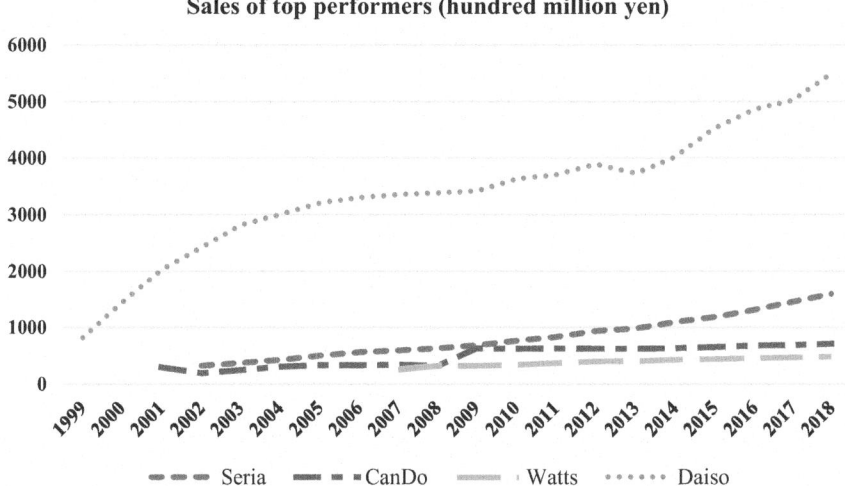

Fig. 4.8 Sales per shop of top 100-yen companies. *Source* Author's calculation from websites of Daiso and annual reports of Seria, CanDo, and Watts

of different formats of retailing, and the economic downturn. The following section examines the status of 100-yen retail chains and their strategies to stay competitive in the stagnant economy and in the face of intense competition (Fig. 4.8).

In terms of growth of total sales, Daiso is in a competitive position as the vanguard of 100-yen retail chains. It is shown in the graph that annual sales of the top performers increased over the period. Growth of sales of these companies is sometimes interrupted by internal and external forces; for example, supply of capital, debt ratio, availability of on-demand products, effective inventory system, frequent changes of retail law, ability to comply with the new amendments of retail law, growth of household income, host country trade and investment policies, and culture of host country (Hitt et al., 2013).

Figure 4.9 shows the sales per shop of top performers for about two decades. Sales per shop for all top companies increased over the stipulated period, with few fluctuations. Daiso is also in the top position in terms of sales per shop relative to other performers. Daiso is the top-ranked company among 100-yen retail chains in terms of growth of capital, total assets, number of employees, number of shops, number of products, and number of overseas operations (Shared Research, 2018). In these terms, Seria, CanDo, and Watts were positioned second, third, and fourth, respectively, with slight fluctuations. Hitt et al. (2013) mentioned that sales per shop might vary from one company to another because of the attractiveness of shop location, local competitors, new entrants in the market, and variations in consumer needs.

Sales growth of the top 100-yen performers is driven by store counts, gross sales, and sales per store. Number of stores, gross sales, and sales per store of Seria have been increasing gradually from its birth. This expansion is the result of Seria's product line-up, based on special theme stores, named "Color the Day" to attract women

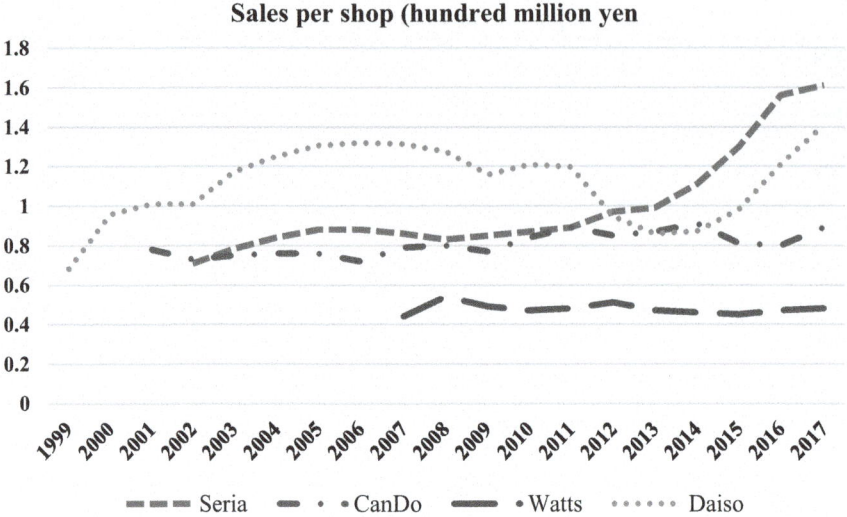

Fig. 4.9 Trends in sales of top 100-yen companies. *Source* Author's calculation from the websites of Daiso and annual reports of Seria, CanDo, and Watts

and students with natural, stylish, and simple products, an advanced technology-based ordering support system, active collaboration with manufacturers in design of products and production, promotion of online sales, and success in developing new stores. Daiso sales have risen rapidly, but its sales per store have fallen in the mid-2010s. Daiso's sales per shop depend not only on domestic shops but also on the success of a large number of overseas stores. Sales of both CanDo and Watts have risen slowly, but sales per store have been trending downward for both companies (Fig. 4.10).

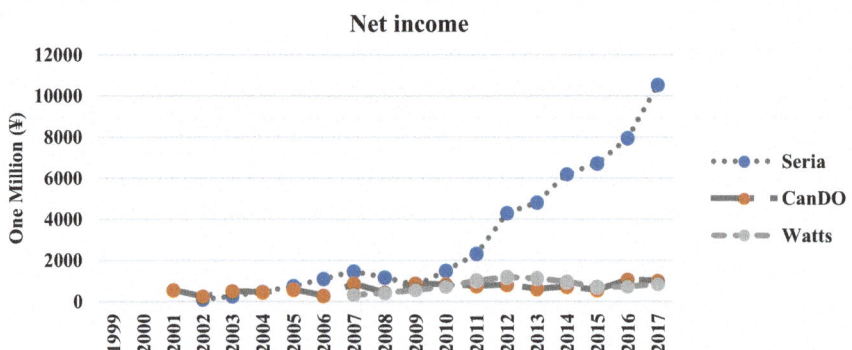

Fig. 4.10 Trends in Net Income (In this case "net income" refers the residual amount of earnings after all expenses have been deducted from sales.) of top 100-yen companies. *Source* Author's calculation from annual reports of Seria, CanDo, and Watts

4.6 Fierce Competition Within 100-Yen Retail Chains

The Fig. 4.10 shows that Seria increased its net income from 2002 to 2007. There was a sharp fall from 2008 to 2009, after which Seria resumed its rising profit until 2017. On the other hand, there were small ups and downs in the net profits of both CanDo and Watts from 2001 to 2017. Nonetheless, the profit trend of Seria, as a second performer, climbed sharply after 2013 because of the dramatic increase in its number of shops from 2012 relative to its competitors. Hitt et al. (2013) noted that companies' profit growth depends significantly on economies of scale, where every company must ensure maximum production and minimum cost. Such being the case, 100-yen companies are struggling to source low-cost products, and the profit rate of these companies mainly depends on cost leadership strategy.

Figure 4.11 outlines the trends in profits per sales of top 100-yen retail shops. Seria increased its profit margin dramatically, from the beginning of the 2010s, and the rate of profit peaked at about 7%. There were small differences between the three performers, from the beginning of the 2000s to the mid-2000s. However, the ratio of profit per sale started to rise dramatically from 2011 and the margin of profit per sale peaked at approximately 7% in 2018. The margin of profit for both CanDo and Watts fluctuated over the stipulated period, from 2001 to early 2018 but remained under 3%. Profit and sales of 100-yen companies are not confined to the sales of 100-yen fixed-price products. Rather, these companies earn profits from retail sales of multi-price products, apart from 100-yen fixed-price products, wholesales, and franchising. The official website of Seria, as well as its annual report (2013), shows that the introduction and application of a proprietary ordering support system in Seria intensified the sales of relatively profitable sundries, lowered the ratio of franchised stores, and cut costs by providing information to suppliers. Seria also attracted repeat customers away from competitors. As well, it maintained higher sales at existing stores and lowered the selling, general, and administrative (SG&A) costs more than its competitors. In summary, attracting repeat customers, using more cutting-edge technology than its competitors, offering both store sales and online sales, selling

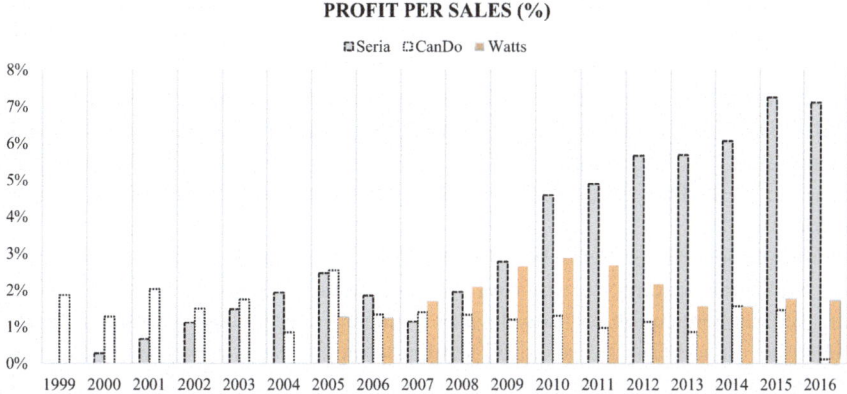

Fig. 4.11 Profit per sales of top 100-yen companies. *Source* Author's calculation from annual reports of Seria, CanDo, and Watts

multi-price products, and targeting segmented customer groups with stylish and natural sundries increased the profit margin of Seria relative to that of competitors.

In the above figures, it is clearly visible that growth in financial performance of 100-yen companies is not static over a given period and varies from one company to another. The main reasons for this variation are each company's distinctive product strategy, corporate strategic plan, the target customer group, business expansion plan, and procurement plan.

Flath (1990) found that Japan's highly developed wholesaling network and goods originating in geographically compact Japan both work to expand the multitude of tiny stores. He also noted that there is a larger variety of retail stores in Japan compared to the U.S. and virtually all European countries. These retail formats are identified by distinct features: for example, convenience stores provide 24-h nonstop service and have diverse services apart from a variegated product line; drugstores satisfy the need not only for medical products but also for daily necessities; and there are numerous other variations, in terms of products and services, across various types of retailing.

The 100-yen chain store is also a widely featured retailer in Japan, recognizable mostly for its distinctive low-cost strategy. It has been found that, against a backdrop of deflation, yen appreciation, and relatively low-cost labor in China after the 1990s, the 100-yen retail chains learned to procure and sell products at low prices. This also increased the consumer demand for low-price items. These stores grew by taking market shares away from supermarkets for household goods and personal effects. After Japan's economic bubble burst, rapid deflation prompted a sharp increase in the number of 100-yen stores and 100-yen retail chains became a growth industry in the 1990s in Japanese retailing. During this period, yen depreciation around the Asian currency crisis of 1998 led to an industry shakeout. The result was an oligopolistic market with four major 100-yen players: Daiso, Seria, CanDo, and Watts.

Yamamoto and Whang (2018) indicated that Daiso strategically adapted its operation to the changes in foreign exchange rates and local demands. To be price competitive outside Japan, Daiso directly distributed products from manufacturing plants to its stores located outside of the country rather than using the Japanese RDCs as delivery hubs. Moreover, some of Daiso's later stores modified the treasury hunt business model and aimed to provide a selected number of specialty products. As of 2016, Daiso had yet to achieve meaningful levels of online sales. Yamamoto and Whang (2018) also added that Daiso's most prominent competitor was Seria, which had advanced the POS system in 2004[6] and had been investing in technology to meet the competition.

Seria introduced the Seria Web-Electric Data Interchange System, connecting itself with manufacturers to improve the merchandise turnover ratio, as well as palm-vein authentication security devices to manage employees' work hours more efficiently.[7] In addition, Seria started selling online, and major competitors among 100-yen chains now are offering multi-price products to compete with other retail

---

[6] Seria Company Data.

[7] Ibid.

formats. According to Yamamoto and Whang (2018), Daiso founder and President Hirotake Yano commented that growth of the company has been achieved solely through constant trial and error and learning from mistakes since the company was founded. He also said that, from its birth, the main theme of the company was survival, and not growth.

Overall, the new trend of retailers in Japan which is the 100-yen retail chain, at the beginning of the 1990s does not see its stores as places where goods of low quality and low value are sold. Based on its strength of buying in large volume, it is constantly surprising with products that are deemed too high in value to be sold at the fixed price of only 100 yen.

Although this section did a trend analysis to investigate the dynamics of the Japanese retail industry, we could not cover the discussion about determinants of the number of retailers across Japan. To investigate this issue, the subsequent section is followed by a social optimal model (Flath, 1990) and spatial competition model (Capozza and Van Order, 1978) for building a regression model which explores the factors determining retail chain density in Japan.

References

Capozza, D.R., & Order, R.V. (1978). A generalized model of spatial competition. *The American Economic Review*, *68*(5), 896–908.
Flath, D. (1990). Why are there so many retail stores in Japan. *Japan and the World Economy, 2*, 365–386.
Flath, D., & Nariu, T. (1996). Is Japan's retail sector truly distinctive? *Journal of Comparative Economics, 23*(2), 181–191.
Heng, S.-H.M. (2009). *Insights from Japan's "Lost Decade"* (Working Paper No., 154). EAI.
Hitt, M.A., Ireland, R.D., & Hoskisson, R.E. (2013). *Strategic management: Competitiveness and globalization* (10th ed.). Mason, Ohio: Thomson/South-Western, pp. 42–60.
Horioka, Y.C. (2004). *The stagnation of household consumption in Japan*. Presented in Institute of Social and Economic Research, Osaka University, Osaka, Japan, and National Bureau of Economic Research, Inc., Cambridge, Massachusetts, USA.
Horioka, Y.C. (2006). The causes of Japan's 'lost decade': The role of household consumption (Discussion Paper No. 661). The Institute of Social and Economic Research Osaka University.
Katsumi, S. (2014). *The effect of large-scale retailers on price level: Evidence from Japanese data for 1977–1992* (RIETI Discussion Paper Series, 14-E-013).
Lottoanti, M.S. (2010). *The effect of the revised large-scale retail stores law on the Japanese distribution system*. University of Zurich.
Rahman, M. A. (2018). Supply chain management practices on performance of retail enterprises: Supplier and customer relationship perspective of 100-yen shops in Japan. *The Ritsumeikan Economic Review, 67*(1), 45–54.
Shared Research. (2018). Shared Research Inc. Seria. https://sharedresearch.jp/en/2782.
Stockdill, R. (2011). The changing landscape of japanese retailing, inside retail. https://insideretail.com.au/news/the-changing-landscape-of-japanese-retailing-201104.
Tsutsui, W.M., & Mazzotta, S. (2015). The bubble economy and the lost decade: Learning from the Japanese economic experience. *Journal of Global Initiatives: Policy, Pedagogy, Perspective*, *9*(1). https://digitalcommons.kennesaw.edu/jgi/vol9/iss1/6.
Yamamoto, K., & Whang, J. (2018). *Daiso of Japan: The dollar store*. Stanford Graduate School of Business Case: GS-90.

Chapter 5
Dollar Stores: A Sense of Small Neighborhoods in the USA

5.1 Background of Dollar Stores

Dollar General is the pioneer in American one-dollar stores offering a wide selection of everyday items with seasonal, closeout, and promotional merchandise. The concept of merchandising commodities at $1 began in 1939 as a family-owned business called J.L. Turner and Son, in Kentucky. In 1955 the name was changed to Dollar General Corporation.[1] Dollar Tree and Family Dollar started merchandising in 1953 and 1958 by the names of K.R. Penny and Ben Franklin variety store Coma and Family Dollar stores, respectively. Gradually, these stores went public and offered a variety of products across the USA after the 1970s.[2]

The retail structure for food, desserts, beverages, and personal and household goods is growing fast because of the rapid innovations in retail formats and changes in consumer preferences. Dollar Stores appeal to limited and fixed-income consumers. Dollar Stores are experiencing rapid growth with more than 10,000 outlets opening over the past decade with plans for continued expansion. The key to the success of Dollar Stores is a strategic focus on poverty.[3] Dollar Stores has shifted from one-price stores to multi-price-point stores to stay competitive with big box retailers like Walmart. The growth of these multi-price stores is faster than that of traditional channels, particularly with regard to personal goods, household goods, food, and beverages, since Dollar Stores offer more variations in food and beverages and the consumer perception of store brand quality has improved.[4]

As the acceptance of online shopping is increasing worldwide, some large retailers in the USA, like Sears and JC Penney, have closed many of their stores, whereas Dollar Store chains have increased sales and stores over the same period, and these stores are creating a good imagine in small communities.

---

[1] DG History, https://newscenter.dollargeneral.com/company-facts/history.

[2] History: The Dollar Tree Story, https://www.dollartree.com/history.

[3] Michael Sainato, October 1, 2019, How Dollar Stores Prey on the Poor, The Progressive Magazine.

[4] Dollar Stores Impacts, Institute for Local Self-Reliance.

5.2 Size of the Stores

Dollar General and Dollar Tree (along with Family Dollar stores from January 2015) manage approximately 17,000 and 15,000 stores and have 2020 net sales of $33.75 billion and $25.5 billion, respectively.[5] Dollar Tree serves the contiguous United States (except for Montana and Idaho) and had a net income of $1.712 billion and 143,000 employeesin 2019. In the same year, Dollar General served the United States and Canada with a net income of $1.714 billion 193,100 employees. These statistics ranked Dollar General *91* and Dollar Tree *111* on the Fortune 500 list of 2021. Overall, Dollar Stores tend to be small in size, making them easy to manage. The average size of Dollar Stores is 8,000 to 12,000 square feet. In January 2015, Dollar Tree outbid Dollar General to acquire the Family Dollar brand for $9.2 billion, thus doubling its size.

5.3 Location of Stores

Dollar Stores are among the fastest growing sectors in retail (Meyersohn, 2021; Meyersohn, 2021a; Lee, 2021). The growth of these stores is attributed to the economies of their small store size; rising income inequality in the United States, accelerated by the Great Recession; and the decline of traditional grocery stores and under-served urban communities (Meyersohn, 2021a; Lee, 2021; Cain, 2020; Wahba, 2019). *The Economist* (2018) and Grigsby et al. (2021) mentioned that Dollar Stores were predominantly located in the South and Midwest in the early 2000s. The presence of Dollar Store growth is most significant in the West and Northeast regions, where Dollar Store counts grew by approximately 51 and 17% on a year-by-year basis (Grigsby et al., 2021).[6]

Recent trends of Dollar Stores across the United States indicate that food retailers are increasingly exposed to Dollar Store competition and that consumers have greater access to Dollar Store retailers. Figure 5.1 shows how Dollar Stores are close to customers and how they are intensely competing with other retailers in the market.

The dominance of Dollar Stores is mostly in rural areas and small towns, where the average distance to the nearest Dollar Store tends to range from 5 to 6 miles.[7] Previous studies seem to identify that the expansion of big box stores, such as Walmart, garnered significant attention from policymakers and researchers (Crowley

---

[5] Dollar General Cooperation. 2007–2020 Annual Report, https://investor.dollargeneral.com/web sites/dollargeneral/English/3200/annual-reports.html.

[6] Grigsby et al. (2021), The Geography of Dollar Stores, Agricultural & Applied Economics Association Annual Meeting, Austin, TX, August 1–August 3.

[7] Grigsby et al. (2021), The Geography of Dollar Stores, Agricultural & Applied Economics Association Annual Meeting, Austin, TX, August 1–August 3.

5.3 Location of Stores

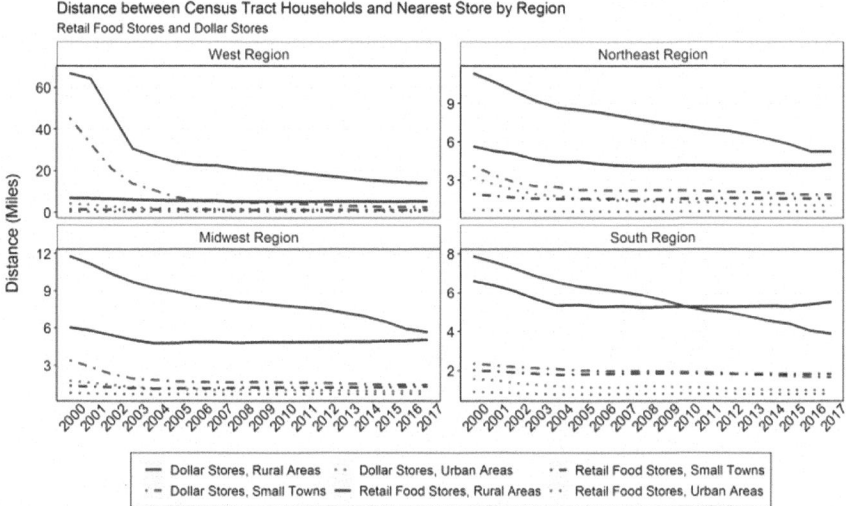

Fig. 5.1 Dollar Store proximity and competition with food retailers. *Source* Chuck Grigsby et al. (2021), The Geography of Dollar Stores

and Stainback, 2019; Hortaçsu and Syverson, 2015[8]; Bonanno and Goetz, 2012). Small-box Dollar Stores also have grown alongside the supercenter and wholesale-club store formats.[9] In some cities, like Tulsa, Oklahoma, people are protesting the expansion of Dollar Stores by city dwellers in the belief that the drastic expansion of Dollar Stores is depriving them of the consumption of fresh foods and necessary commodities.

Dollar Stores have been increasing in the last decade across the 50 states of the USA. Focused location, low cost, non-durable diversified products, and the economic recession have resulted in the rise of Dollar Stores steadily over that period. The unusual growth of these stores is the biggest challenge for individual grocery stores and the health of people in the community, since Dollar Stores have focused on frozen products, ignoring fresh and green foods (Fig. 5.2).

---

[8] Hortaçsu and Syverson (2015), The Ongoing Evolution of US Retail: A Format Tug-of-War, NBER Working Paper Series.

[9] Grigsby et al. (2021), The Geography of Dollar Stores, Agricultural & Applied Economics Association Annual Meeting, Austin, TX, August 1–August 3.

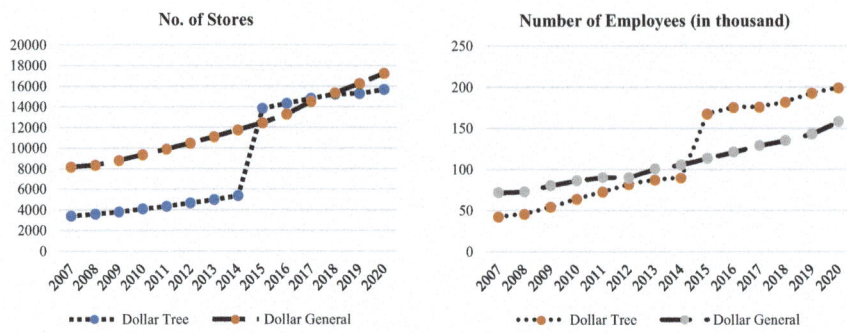

Fig. 5.2 Number of stores and number of employees. *Source* Dollar General and Dollar Tree

5.4 How Dollar Stores Are Competing

Dollar Stores aim to serve customers with everyday low-price merchandise in convenient locations and easy-to-navigate store layouts. Dollar Stores have expanded in the last decade because of the stagnant economy and by adapting their strategy to the community, which are shown in the following framework (Fig. 5.3).

5.5 Dollar Stores Create a Sense of Community

Dollar Stores are mainly prevalent in low-income neighborhoods. The number of Dollar Stores is increasing rapidly across the United States with the appeal of everyday low-price household products. These stores have replaced full-service grocery stores and led to the closure of independent stores in some of the most impoverished neighborhoods. For example, the poorest areas of North Tulsa, Oklahoma, have dozens of Dollar Stores but not a single full-service grocery store.[10] Expansion of Dollar Stores in Texas, Louisiana, and Oklahoma shows no sign of stopping. Because of the following reasons, Dollar Stores are acquiring an image of specialty retail stores in some areas of the United States.

- Low-income neighborhoods and communities of color are saturated with small retail food outlets. Dollar Stores target communities of color, where grocery store chains underinvest. Predominantly, white communities have two to four times more large grocery stores than do communities of color.
- Dollar General focuses on white communities whereas Family Dollar and Dollar Tree concentrate on communities of color. Three quarters of Dollar General Stores

---

[10] Stacy Mitchel and Maarie Donahue (6 December 2018), Report: Dollar Stores are targeting Struggling Urban Neighborhoods and Small Towns. One Community Is Showing How to Fight Back.

5.5 Dollar Stores Create a Sense of Community

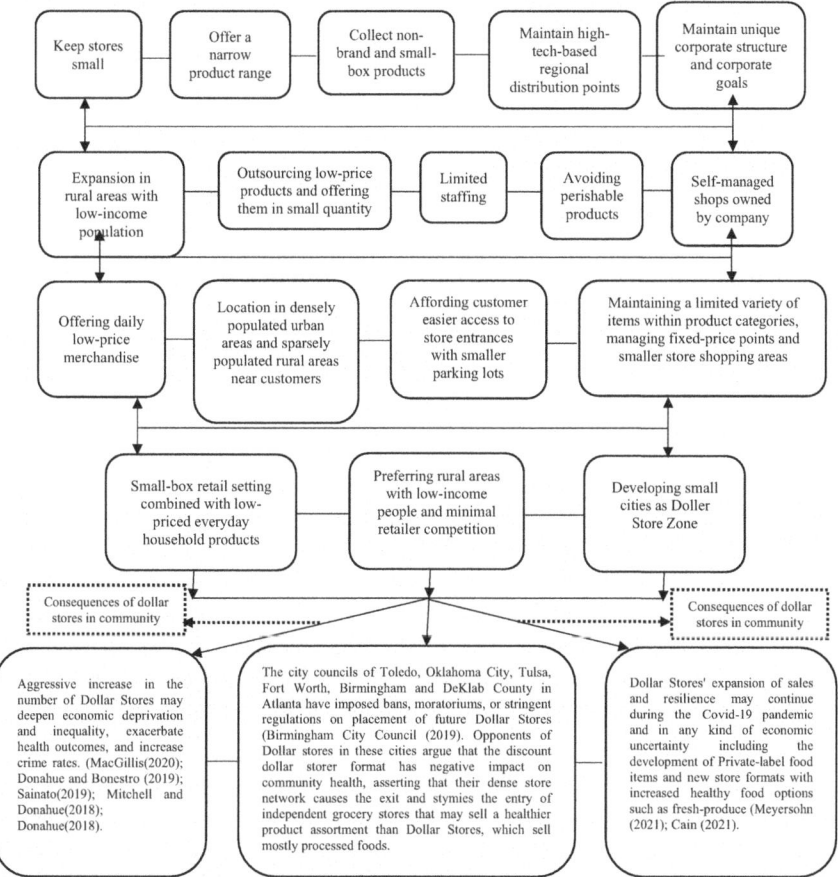

Fig. 5.3 Dollar Stores' strategies and the consequences to the community. *Source* Dollar General and Dollar Tree and literature from previous studies

are located in communities of 20,000 or fewer people. These locations are often 15 to 20 miles away from a full-service grocery store.
- The Supplemental Nutrition Assistance Program (SNAP) has been a key component of Dollar Stores' expansion strategy since the 2008 recession. Between 2007 and 2017, the total number of SNAP-authorized stores increased from 162,000 to 250,000; the U.S. Government Accountability Office attributes much of the increase to limited-service retailers such as Dollar Stores.[11]
- A significant portion of Dollar General's customers lives in households that earn less than $149,900 annually. An executive of Dollar General (DG) explained to

---
[11] The Rise of Dollar Stores: How the Proliferation of Discount Stores May Limit Healthy Food Access, Centre for Science in the Public Interest.

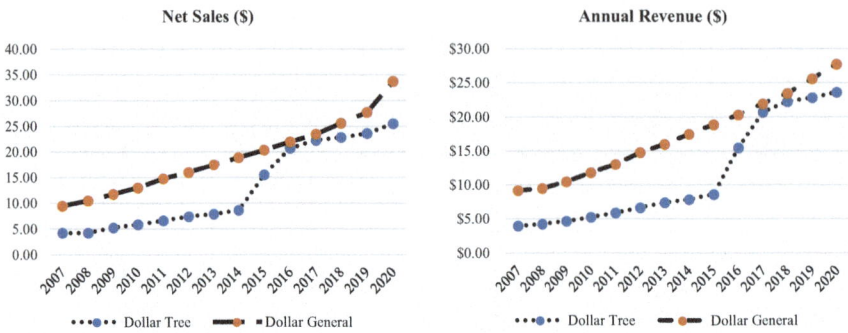

Fig. 5.4 Net sales and annual revenue. *Source* Dollar Tree and Dollar General

investors that in DG's core customer base, households making under $35,000 and reliant on government assistance are the stores' "best friends forever".[12]

- Dollar Stores mainly offer processed and non-perishable food, not fresh produce. Only 3% of DG's more than 18,000 stores currently offer fresh produce. Pressure from community and public health advocates may be changing the scenario. Dollar General launched DG Fresh in some communities recently which serve as an initiative to ensure more fresh produce for customers. Dollar General also has started investing in cold storage and distribution for perishables, which can provoke competitors of Dollar General to stay competitive (Fig. 5.4).

Annual net sales and revenue of both Dollar Tree and Dollar General have been escalating steadily. Dollar General, Dollar Tree, and Family Dollar (owned by Dollar Tree) made up 70% of the grocery market by 2020 in the US. Dollar General outranked Coca-Cola on the Fortune 100 after a rampant increase of revenue by 22%.[13] Both Dollar Tree and Dollar General earn an average gross profit of $0.30 for every $1 in sales, and this rate is higher than rivals of leading Dollar Stores like Target ($0.28) and Walmart ($0.24). Dollar stores are gaining profit by going after the goods nobody else wants, like surplus items, discontinued products, and old stock that did not sell well elsewhere.

In conclusion, Dollar Stores are designed to get customers to spend more money, from keeping product sizes small to stocking private-label merchandise. It has been the sense of binding a good deal to a significant part of US communities.

---

[12] Why Dollar Stores are Bad Business for the Neighborhoods They Open In. https://www.fastcompany.com/90278384/why-dollar-stores-are-bad-business-for-the-neighborhoods-they-open-in.

[13] The economics of dollar stores (June 26, 2021), Zachary Crockett.

5.6 Adverse Effects of Dollar Stores on a Community

1. Dollar Stores have concentrated on providing processed, packed, and non-perishable products to communities, which leads to depriving customers of fresh foods and necessary nutrition. This business strategy of Dollar Stores is a barrier to their further expansion in some cities like Tulsa, Oklahoma.
2. It has been claimed that Dollar Stores have cut sales at supermarkets by about 30% in small towns that are often served by a single, locally owned supermarket. Prompt expansion of Dollar Stores in African American communities results in a sharp decrease in sales and revenue of supermarkets, which puts grocery stores out of business and causes them to leave the community.

5.6.1 Dollar Stores' Employee Management and Exploitation of Workers

Dollar Stores create employment for fewer people than the grocery stores they eliminate. For example, Dollar General outlets have 9 staff members on average whereas small independent grocery stores employ an average of 14.

Dollar Stores jobs are not only fewer in number but also are low-wage and low-quality. Employees are monitored intensely and subject to a "web of contradictory work policies". Court records reveal that Dollar chains frequently face class-action lawsuits for violating fair labor laws, typically paying millions to settle such suits in court. These companies also depend heavily on taxpayers to subsidize their employees' healthcare.

Dollar Stores hire employees for managing stores on both a temporary and permanent basis but their positions are not classified as managerial jobs. An individual employee is responsible for performing various jobs without any specific job description or job classification. Jobs of individual employees include unloading trucks, processing freight, scouring toilets, running cash registers, cleaning, shelving, changing prices, taking inventory, and covering for other employees.

Dollar Store companies routinely classify regular workers as managers in order to categorize them as employees who are not subject to the overtime provisions of the 1938 Fair Labor Standards Act (FLSA).[14]

To sell cheap products and gain more profits, these stores import products from sweatshops in low-wage countries including China, Vietnam, Bangladesh, Cambodia, and Mexico. It is also reported that Dollar Stores including Dollar Tree and Dollar General extract super-profits from the uncompensated labor and overworked store "managers" and other employees. Depriving employees from fair wages, maintaining supply chains with sweatshops, and treating employees inappropriately are evidence of exploiting workers not only in their home countries but all over the globe.

---

[14] Kent Paterson (2010), Dollar Stores: Top Link in the Sweatshop Chain, https://www.corpwatch.org/article/dollar-stores-top-link-sweatshop-chain.

References

Bonanno, A., & Goetz, J. S. (2012). WalMart and local economic development: A survey. *Economic Development Quarterly, 26*(4), 285–297.

Cain, A. (2020). *"Dollar General's push to fill stores with fresh produce and frozen-food options gives the chain a big box feel"*, Insider. https://www.businessinsider.com/dollar-general-dg-fresh-grocery-2020-8.

Crowley, M., & Stainback, K. (2019). Retail sector concentration, local economic structure, and community well-being. *Annual Review of Sociology, 45*(1), 321–343. https://doi.org/10.1146/annurev-soc-073018-022449.

Hortaçsu, A., & Syverson, C. (2015). The ongoing evolution of US retail: A format Tug-of-War. *The Journal of Economic Perspectives, 29*(4), 89–111. http://www.jstor.org/stable/43611012.

Lee, J. (2021). *"Dollar stores deserve a break; Dollar General gave muted guidance for 2021 but there are plenty of tailwinds that should help its main customer base"*.

Meyersohn, N. (2021). *"Dollar tree will soon be the $1.25 store, CNN Business"*. https://news.lee.net/news/national/dollar-tree-will-soon-be-the-1-25-store/article_644a9fb0-4c8a-11ec-b12a-9f9d473d0dce.html.

Meyersohn, N. (2021a). *"Nearly 1 in 3 new stores opening in the US is a Dollar General"*, CNN Business. https://edition.cnn.com/2021/05/06/business/dollar-store-openings-retail/index.html.

Wahba, P. (2019). *Making billions at the dollar store.* https://fortune.com/longform/dollar-general-billions-revenue.

Chapter 6
Determinants of Retail Chain Diversity in Japan

Ministry of Economy, Trade, and Industry (METI), Japan distinguishes eight major business sectors in retailing which are department stores, general merchandise stores, specialty merchandise, convenience stores, drugstores, other specialty stores, specialty stores (apparel, food, household), and semi-specialty stores (apparel, food, household). This section discusses about how and why Japanese retail market became diversified with numerous types of retail chain. We have discussed here gradual expansion of diversified Japanese retail market in accordance with periodical changes.

6.1 Development of Diverse Retail Chain in Japan

At the beginning of the 1900s, rapid increases in the populations and incomes in urban areas, and the overall development of the railway network forced people living in rural areas to travel into the cities to shop and so on. These changes led to the appearance of department stores as a new format of retail business in Japan. The growth of department stores rose steadily starting in the 1930s. These larger and fascinating stores offered a wide selection of Japanese and Western products to attract many customers, and this first retail chain exposed itself to the customer as "the place to spend time." Meyer-Ohle (2003) mentioned that tremendous changes have been taking place over the past 50 years in Japanese retailing, although some elements of it appeared traditional and somewhat outdated at first sight. New retail techniques and retail formats have been introduced continuously. Meyer-Ohle (2003) also explained that many innovations in Japanese retailing were borrowed from Western countries and were inspired by developments in foreign countries, and quite a few occurred within Japan.

The 1950s saw the first technological innovation, *cash registers*, in Japan's retail industry, and this decade also experienced increases in the incomes of salaried worker households, with a steady increase in the average per-capita income of Japanese people. These changes brought the introduction of new retail techniques culminating in the formation of several new retail formats in the 1950s and 1960s. General merchandise stores (GMS) chains have been the most widely used retailers as well as the most innovative once since the 1960s. GMS chains operate large retail stores, second in size only to department stores, and both of these important store formats are operated by some of the largest retail companies. Daiei, Ito-Yokado, Aeon, Seiyu, and Uny are the leading five chains in this sector. Being the pioneer in this regard, Daiei followed this concept further and operated six superstores, introducing its own brand in 1961. Operators of the GMSs entered a period of the rapid expansion of retail sales through the phases of the introduction and formation of the superstore format. This period of retail innovation in Japan can be characterized by the following developments Meyer-Ohle (2003):

- Development of new locations, especially in the rapidly expanding dormitory suburbs of Tokyo
- Construction of shopping centers with superstores
- Expansion of sales floors: new stores that opened after 1965 averaged sales floors of more than 1500 m^2; after 1969, this increased to 3000–5000 m^2, with single stores reaching sizes of up to 7500 m^2.
- Introduction of elements such as self-service, self-choice, and centralized payment in various product categories
- Gradual broadening of assortments through the addition of new product lines

Overall, the period saw the continued development of the general superstore with the enlargement of sales floors and the addition of amenities and services. At the beginning of the 1970s, most stores were integrated into so called shopping centers. Although called shopping centers, these shopping complexes were relatively small overall, and each had only one anchor tenant that heavily dominated the complex. Even though the number of shopping centers reached the number of 1695 by the end of 1992, their average size was only 11,322 m^2 (Larke & Causton, 2005), of which the key tenant occupied 4761 m^2, and an average of 46 other tenants shared about 3955 m^2 (JCSC,[1] 1993).

Larke and Causton (2005) explained that the intensified competition in the 1970s between the operators of general superstores and the beginning saturation of certain regional markets also led to escalated efforts to expand the scope of operations. Companies in this period expanded their store networks as far as the relatively remote areas of Northern Japan and Hokkaido. Their initiatives were supported by the convergence of consumption patterns in rural and urban areas. Although significant differences in lifestyles and incomes between urban and rural areas existed until

---

[1] Japan Council of Shopping Centers (JCSC) was established in April 1973 to promote better lifestyles for consumers and to stimulate local communities through the development of shopping centers. http://www.jcsc.or.jp/sc_english/.

the oil crisis, these differences gradually declined during the 1970s through productivity increases, the government-guaranteed income in agriculture, and a slowdown of growth in the secondary industries. This period also experienced a gradual increase in prosperity in rural areas, which led to a high rate of car ownership with increasing mobility, and Western consumer goods were increasingly introduced into rural areas.

In the 1990s, low growth rates, rising unemployment, and a growing number of bankruptcies characterized a prolonged period of structural change and led to a lengthy slump in the market. Deregulations, such as the large-scale retail store law (LSRSL), brought about changes in the competitive retail environment after the bubble period (1990s). The consequences of revised retail laws after the 1990s led to an increase in the number of retail chains with structured floor sizes. This period saw the expansion of specialty retail stores, such as hole electrical appliances, home centers, drug stores, convenience stores, 100-yen shops, etc. This period also experienced the expansion of large suburban shopping centers.

The 2000s accelerated the low birthrate in Japan and expanded the aging society, which resulted in lower employment in the establishments. In addition, the stagnation of economic growth and rising fierce competition propelled Japanese retailers to explore the new method of retailing. Consequently, the 2010s have witnessed the pursuit of the expansion of neighborhood shopping centers, JR-station stores, and online shopping.

6.2 Impact of Socio-Economic Factors on Retail Density

6.2.1 Descriptive Statistics

Descriptive statistics enable us to explore the data at our disposal. We used 141 observations across Japan to investigate the determinants of retail density (Table 6.1).

Table 6.2 shows the Spearman's rank correlation to reduce any distortions among variables. We picked Spearman's Rank Correlation over Pearson's because the latter can unfortunately be prone to influence by outliers and other factors, such as unequal variances.

Table 6.1 Summary of statistics

Name of variable	Observations	Mean	Std. Dev	Min	Max
DPoP	141	671.54	1183.433	64.51	6416.807
S_Stores	141	139.03	32.08	2.84	221.78
S_Houses	141	108.04	19.46	63.94	156.54
Cars	141	0.55	0.16	0.25	0.89

Table 6.2 Spearman's correlation coefficient

Variables	Correlation coefficient between variables			
Density of Population	1.0000			
Size of stores	0.0590	1.0000		
Size of houses	−0.5486	0.0839	1.0000	
Number of cars	−0.3152	0.7255	0.3976	1.0000

6.2.2 Empirical Estimation

In accordance with the Hausman test, the fixed effect model is more appropriate for investigating the socio-economic effects on the retail density of Japan. The probability of the Hausman specification test (1978) for this study is Prob > chi2 = 0.000. Although the Hausman test recommends adopting the fixed effect model for examining our hypothesis, the estimated result of the fixed effect model (Appendix 1) is not well suited for the hypothesis of this study. Gujrati (2004) recommended that the fixed effect model is convenient for longitudinal panel data, but this study was confined to three years of cross-sectional data, which were transformed into panel data for more sample variability. We adopted both the ordinary least square model and the random effect model.

Density of total retailers (LTR_Stores)

The OLS result shows that independent variables are significant except for LS_Stores. On the other hand, REM estimates our hypothesis, where all explanatory variables have a significant impact on the density of total retailers in Japan. The estimated results show that the increase of the population intensifies the number of chain stores, but the statistical data of MLITT and METI show that both the population and the number of total retailers in Japan decreased gradually during the period of the 1990s to 2010s. The increasing sizes of stores, sizes of houses, and number of cars can decrease the number of total retailers.

Density of 100-yen Chain shops (L100_yen_shops)

For L100_yen chain shops, only OLS is available due to the existence of one year of data on the total number of 100-yen retail chain establishments. The results reveal that the density of 100-yen shops can vary across Japan in terms of the density of the population, the sizes of stores, the sizes of houses, and the number of cars. In this case, the coefficient of all predictors is positive except for sizes of houses. In terms of 100-yen shops, the absolute value of the coefficient on LS_House is high and inversely significant, which is consistent with our analytical model. In this regard, only the restoring and reordering costs of customers are significant for the expansion of 100-yen shops.

6.2 Impact of Socio-Economic Factors on Retail Density 65

Density of Chain Supermarkets (LSuper_Mkts)

The LSuper_Mkts estimates for OLS regression found that the density of the population and the sizes of houses have a significant effect on the number of supermarkets in Japan. On the other hand, the estimation of the REM reveals that the density of the population and the number of cars only have an impact on the number of supermarkets. Here, the coefficient value of cars per person describes a negative relationship between LCars and retail chain density, which is consistent with our analytical model. This means that consumers are likely to shop in supermarkets using cars and that transportation costs would have a large impact on diverse supermarkets in this sense. The sizes of stores and sizes of houses are insignificant for the expansion of supermarkets, which is inconsistent with our assumption. This means that restocking and reordering costs may not have an impact on the density of supermarkets.

Density of other Chain Supermarkets (LOther_SMkts)

The examination of LOther_SMkts estimates for both OLS and the REM finds almost the same effect of explanatory variables on the response variables of this study. LDPoP, LS_Houses, and LCars have significant relationships with the number of other retailers in Japan. The coefficients of significant predictors are negative except for LDPoP. Both transportation and restocking costs might have a significant impact on the number of other supermarkets, such as specialty supermarkets and clothing supermarkets. A few specialty supermarkets are found in densely inhabited areas, where shoppers travel using cars as the means of convenient transportation. Gradual increases in the sizes of houses and the proliferation of cars would decrease the number of other supermarkets, which is consistent with our analytical model.

Density of Chain Drug Stores (LD_Stores)

The estimated results for both OLS and the REM identified that LDPoP and LS_Houses have significant impacts on the number of drug stores in Japan. Transportation cost does not have any influence on the expansion of drug store chains because the coefficient value of car per person remains insignificant for determining the number of drug stores, whereas restocking and reordering costs are significant modifiers for the determination of drug stores.

Density of Chain Convenient Stores (LC_Stores)

The OLS result shows that LDPoP and LS_Houses have an effect on the number of convenient store chains in Japan. On the contrary, the examination of estimates for the REM finds the significant impact of LDPoP, LS_Houses, and LCars on the density of convenient stores in Japan. The coefficient value of significant estimates for the REM are negative except for LDPoP, which implies that the number of convenient stores depends on the restocking cost and transportation cost of the consumer, which is allied with our analytical model.

6.2.3 Effect of Large-Scale Store Law on Retail Chain Density After the 1990s

Previous studies Flath (1990), Potjes et al. (1992), Matsui and Yukimoto (2004) include number of department stores (Dept_Store) per household as the key variable to examine the effects of Large-Scale Retail Sore Law (LSRSL) on the density of retail stores in Japan. Previous studies considered number of department stores per household as an indication of the severity of local application of the LSRSL. We also adapted the variable "Dept_Store" to examine the intensity of LSRSL application on the density of retail chain stores after the 1990s. Table 6.4 shows the results of the effect of LSRSL on retail chain density along with the effect of socio-economic factors (Table 6.3).

The OLS results of this study show positive significant coefficient in terms of total retailers and all types of chain stores rather than 100-yen shops which presume that proliferation of department stores can increase the number of other retail chain stores. Nevertheless, the real scenario of department stores and others chain stores is contrary with the result of our empirical study. The following graph shows the present scenario of department store in Japan (Fig. 6.1).

Though the coefficients of this study show the positive significant impact on the density of retail chain stores, the actual scenario of the retail chain stores is vis-a vis in accordance with the statistics of METI. The question is why actual scenario and the result of this study are different. The department store law (DSL) was enacted in the 1950s to protect small retailers from the competition of department stores. The key aim of this law was ensuring business opportunities for small- and medium-sized retailers by regulating the business operations of department stores the DSL prohibited the operation of a "department store business" with more than 1500 m^2 ("m^2") of retail space unless the store obtained a permit from METI.[2]

The government of Japan enacted large stores law (LSL) in 1973 which was recognized as large scale retail store law later. Instead of regulating the type of store, e.g., department stores, the new LSL targeted the amount of retail floor space in a single building, regardless of the legal nature of the stores that it housed. Its purpose was to preserve business opportunities for small- and medium-sized retailers though adjustments of the business activities of large stores.[3]

By the mid-1980s, METI's regulation of large stores was under attack from a variety of sources. Large stores "complained" about the arbitrary and often extended prior adjustment process and small retailers were unhappy with the continuing expansion of large stores.[4] Debate on the large store regulation intensified in the mid1980s when foreign complaints began to intrude on what had been predominantly a domestic issue. The LSL moved onto the U.S.-Japan trade agenda, where it would stay for the next fifteen years. The United States raised barriers posed by the LSL for the

---

[2] Frank Upham, Privatizing Regulation: The Implementation of the LargeScale Retail Stores Law, in Political Dynamics, supra note 3, 268–69.

[3] Large Stores Law, Law No. 109 of 1973.

[4] Schoppa (1997), Bargaining with Japan, Supra Note 20, 152.

6.2 Impact of Socio-Economic Factors on Retail Density

Table 6.3 Results of OLS regression and random effect model (REM)

	LTR_Stores		L100_yen_shops	LSuper_Mkts		LOther_SMkts		LD_Stores		LC_Stores	
	OLS	GLS	OLS	OLS	GLS	OLS	GLS	OLS	GLS	OLS	GLS
Cons	11.56 (1.50)	15.47 (1.98)	16.73 (4.59)	8.68 (1.59)	6.49 (2.21)	9.54 (1.93)	10.61 (2.88)	6.76 (2.08)	6.87 (3.12)	9.49 (2.02)	12.33 (2.62)
LDPoP	0.24*** (0.05)	0.14* (0.08)	0.55*** (0.15)	0.28*** (0.05)	0.36*** (0.08)	0.31*** (0.06)	0.31*** (0.10)	0.45*** (0.07)	0.48*** (0.11)	0.37*** (0.07)	0.31*** (0.10)
LS_Stores	0.07 (0.10)	−0.05*** (0.02)	0.73** (0.31)	0.14 (0.11)	0.00 (0.03)	0.11 (0.13)	−0.04 (0.06)	0.18 (0.14)	0.02 (0.06)	0.13 (0.14)	−0.04 (0.03)
LS_Houses	−0.86*** (0.26)	−1.45*** (0.36)	−3.77*** (0.80)	−0.90*** (0.28)	−0.38 (0.40)	−1.15*** (0.34)	−1.21** (0.53)	−1.08*** (0.36)	−0.96* (0.57)	−1.31*** (0.35)	−1.67*** (0.48)
LCars	−0.78*** (0.15)	−0.77*** (0.03)	6.77*** (0.47)	−0.24 (0.16)	−0.21*** (0.04)	−0.33* (0.20)	−0.24*** (0.08)	−0.10 (0.21)	0.05 (0.08)	−0.33 (0.21)	−0.28*** (0.04)
R^2	0.59	0.94	0.69	0.49	0.40	0.48	0.19	0.52	0.00	0.53	0.57

Dependent Variable: LTR_Stores, L100_yen shops, LSuper_Mkts, LOther_SMkts, LD_Stores, LC_Stores
*** $p < 0.01$, ** $p < 0.05$, * $p < 0.1$, Parentheses are the standard error of the coefficients

Table 6.4 Results of OLS regression and random effect model (REM)

	LTotal_Retailers		L100_Yen_shop	LSuper_Mkts		LOther_Super_Mkts		LD_Stores		LC_Stores	
	OLS	GLS	OLS	OLS	GLS	OLS	GLS	OLS	GLS	OLS	GLS
Cons	10.80 (1.18)	14.46 (1.78)	16.52 (4.61)	7.80 (1.18)	7.89 (1.85)	8.59 (1.55)	10.19 (2.41)	5.66 (1.60)	6.83 (2.47)	8.43 (1.55)	11.74 (2.33)
LDoPopu	0.12*** (0.04)	0.16** (0.07)	0.51*** (0.16)	0.14*** (0.04)	0.29*** (0.07)	0.16*** (0.05)	0.27*** (09)	0.27*** (0.06)	0.39*** (0.09)	0.20*** (0.05)	0.31*** (0.09)
LStore_size	−0.05 (0.08)	−0.05** (0.02)	0.70** (0.32)	0.00 (0.08)	−0.00 (0.03)	−0.04 (0.11)	−0.04 (0.06)	−0.00 (0.11)	02 (0.06)	−0.04 (0.11)	−0.04 (0.03)
LHouse_size	−0.52** (0.21)	−1.26*** (33)	−3.68*** (0.82)	−0.51** (0.21)	−0.61* (0.34)	−0.73*** (0.27)	−1.11** (0.44)	−0.59** (0.28)	−0.91** (0.45)	−0.83*** (0.27)	−1.55*** (0.43)
LCars	−0.38*** (0.13)	−0.74*** (0.03)	6.88*** (0.50)	0.22* (0.13)	−0.15*** (0.05)	0.16 (0.17)	−0.16*** (0.10)	0.47*** (0.17)	0.21** (0.10)	0.22 (0.17)	−0.22** (05)
LDept_Store	0.38*** (04)	0.05** (0.02)	0.11 (0.16)	0.44*** (0.04)	0.08*** (0.03)	0.47*** (0.05)	0.12** (0.05)	0.54*** (0.06)	0.21*** (0.05)	0.53*** (0.05)	0.06** (0.03)
R^2	0.75	0.94	0.68	0.72	0.37	0.67	0.12	0.72	0.00	0.72	0.56

6.2 Impact of Socio-Economic Factors on Retail Density

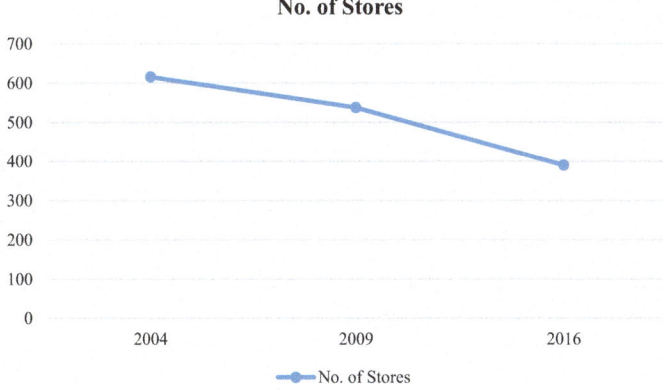

Fig. 6.1 Trends of department stores in Japan. *Source* Authors' calculation based on METI 2004, 2009, and 2016

first time in 1985 at U.S.-Japan Trade Committee meetings. Beginning in 1986, the United States listed the LSL as a "trade barrier" in its annual report to Congress on foreign trade barriers.[5]

METI developed a "Vision for the Distribution Industry" in the 1990s to overcome challenges from various sources regarding retail stores in which it proposed reforms of the retail regulatory mechanism.[6] The reformation of retail store law in the 1990s mainly focused on the size of sales floor and time of retail store operation.[7] It can be assumed from the above discussion that the main purpose of the DSL and the LSRSL was to protect small and medium enterprises of Japan from the severe completion of department stores and to keep the interest of small stores which was dismantled by the internal political pressure and outright interruption of U.S at the end of 1990. Therefore, the impact of the DSL or the LSRSL prevailed only determining the density of total retailers before 1990s. For this reason, the result of this study did not find fruitful empirical results to examine the impact of the DSL or LSRSL on the density of retail chain stores since the floor size of retail chain stores are followed by the provisions of the reformed retail store law at the end of 1990.

---

[5] Schoppa, Supra Note 20, 160–61.

[6] Schoppa, Supra Note 20, 156.

[7] USTR (1989), National Trade Estimate Report of Foreign Trade Barriers 113–14; Schoppa, Supra Note 20, 161–62 (explaining how the barriers that Toys "R" Us faced, as the first large American retailer seeking to enter the Japanese market, allowed the United States to finally make a direct argument that LSL blocked American retailers); Upham, Supra Note 20, 267 (describing how Toys "R" Us' interest in direct participation in the Japanese market allowed the U.S. requests to include pressure on Japan to lift the LSL's barrier on the entry of foreign retailers into Japan).

6.2.4 Discussion

The empirical results of this study vary from one type of retail chain to another, which proves the hypothesis of this study to be consistent in most cases. Variation in empirical results befalls due to the influences of external forces on a large variety of retail chains since the 1950s. Changing to an efficient distribution system from an inefficient one, and shifting the economy from a bubble to a recession had a momentous impact on the socio-economic changes in Japan, which further contributed to determining the density of retail chains in the inhabited areas of Japan. Meyer-Ohle (2003) pointed out that the Japanese distribution system seems to be a prime example of the stable relationships between a variety of chain stores and consumers' shopping behavior.

Although the retail sector has shown some change, the wholesale sector has demonstrated an astonishing pattern of structural constancy that persisted even throughout the 1990s. The underlying reasons for this stability are to be found mainly in the attitudes shown by manufacturers, wholesalers, and retailers toward their positions and roles in the distribution channel. Coordination rather than mobilization was the dominant feature of change in Japanese distribution from manufacturers' dominance to retailers' dominance. Flath (1990) claimed the dualistic economy of Japan to be a prime means of the inefficient distribution sector. Before the 1970s, a large number of small retail stores in Japan showed symptoms of economically wasteful overemployment. Since the 1980s, several shop types started to modernize and became relatively efficient [e.g., department stores, supermarkets, convenience stores, and specialty chain stores].

In addition, the Japanese distribution system of the 1990s has been considered to be a revolutionary change for the retail industry. This transformation was related to the number of factors, most significantly deregulation, the stricter application of fair-trade regulations, changes in consumer behavior, the entry of foreign retailers, and increasing imports through the appreciation of the yen. The most significant and successful change in the distribution channels of Japanese retailing ascended after the introduction of the convenience store. Meyer-Ohle (2003) described that with convenience store companies having proceeded so far already in the organization of their supply chains, Seven-Eleven finally went even one step further. In November 1997, Seven-Eleven organized 25 wholesalers to establish a separate new company with the exclusive purpose of supplying the company's convenience stores with daily miscellaneous goods and sundries. The establishment of this company was its final move to transform a manufactured-oriented distribution structure into a retail-oriented one. Eventually, this newly developed distribution channel was followed by retailers characterized by small sales floors, limited storage space, broad assortments, and long business hours. This innovative distribution channel after the mid-1990s transformed the retail structure and wholesale structure of Japan.

This chapter examines the determinants of retail chain density in Japan. To understand more detail about the retail structure of Japan, the following chapter aims to discuss briefly about the factors affecting changes in the distribution system of Japan.

References

Flath, D. (1990). Why are there so many retail stores in Japan. *Japan and the World Economy, 2,* 365–386.

Gujarati, N. D. (2004). *Basic econometrics.* McGraw Hill, Fourth Edition, pp. 640–642.

Hausman, J. A. (1978). Specification tests in econometrics. *Econometrica, 46,* 1251–1271.

Larke, R., & Causton, M. (2005). *Japan—A modern retail superpower.* Palgrave Macmillan, pp. 225–265.

Matsui, K., & Yukimoto, T. (2004). Retail store density in Japan. *Japanese Economy, 32,* 49–75.

Meyer-Ohle, H. (2003). *Innovation and dynamics in Japanese retailing: From techniques to formats to systems.* New York, NY: Palgrave Macmillan.

Potjes, J. C. A., Carree M. A., & Thurik, A. R. (1992). *Japanese retail stores: Regulation, retailer-client relations and the dual econom*y. Econometric Institute, Erasmus University Rotterdam, Netherlands, Report 9245/A.

Chapter 7
Factors Affecting Changes in Distribution System in Japan

Japanese retail companies adopt distribution strategies to achieve competitive growth. Wholesalers play key role between manufacturers and retailers that is largely determined by the structure of the retail market and is highly dependent on the distribution strategies that are employed by manufacturers and retailers. This section aims to discuss about the basic features of the changes in the Japanese distribution structure and it includes discussion about the factors contributed to change the distribution system of Japan with some graphical analyses. This chapter examines the strategic changes in distribution channel after the 1990s and at the end of this chapter we discuss about the new dynamics in the distribution system of Japan.

7.1 Background of the Japanese Distribution Structure

The Japanese distribution has been entered a period of significant change from the beginning of the 2000s. The structure of the distribution channels that link manufacturers and retailers is largely determined by the structure of the retail market and is highly dependent on the distribution strategies that manufacturers and retailers employ. Distribution structure, mainly, constructed by manufacturers, wholesalers, and retailers. Wholesalers work to aggregate transactions between manufacturers and numerous retail stores that can reduce transaction costs of both parties. Japanese retail companies adopt distribution strategies that rely on the inventory management and delivery functions of wholesalers and have achieved short-term growth by concentrating their management resources in building stores. Previous chapters of this study concentrated on Japanese retail industry which discuss few relevant issues of Japanese distribution channels. This part of our study aims to examine the factors which contributed to change the distribution structure of Japan after the 1990s.

7.2 Basic Features of Changes in Distribution Structure

Meyer-Ohle (2003) pointed out, the Japanese distribution system seems to be a prime example for stable relationships. At least, this is the case in quantitative terms. While the retail sector has shown some change, the wholesale sector has demonstrated an astonishing pattern of structural constancy that persisted even throughout the 1990s. The underlying reasons for this stability are to be found mainly in the attitudes shown by manufacturers, wholesalers and retailers toward their position and role in the distribution channel. On the one hand, manufacturers and, to a smaller extent, wholesalers tried to gain control over other members within distribution channels. On the other hand, big retail companies concentrated efforts not on their purchasing activities but on the development of sales concepts. Above all, actors in Japanese distribution focused on smaller changes and did not aim for drastic reorganization. In terms of distribution system, coordination rather than mobilization was the dominant feature of change in Japanese distribution. There are some distinct features of Japanese distribution channel (JDC) which are discussed in the following paragraphs.

Dual economy: a mean for the inefficiency of the distribution system

Dualistic economy is often claimed as the inefficiency of the distribution system in Japanese retailing. The Japanese economy system is often described to have a dual structure, with both efficient large manufacturing companies and inefficient small-scale manufacturing and service industries Caves and Uekusa (1976), Reischauer (1977). Flath (1990) indicated, Japan has a dualistic economy in which the distribution sector, unlike some other sectors, is economically backwards and riddled with anachronistic customs that have a cultural basis rather than an economic basis. In accordance with this view, the large number of stores in japan is a symptom of economically wasteful overemployment. Since 1960, several shop-types started to modernize and became relatively efficient [e.g. department stores, supermarkets, convenience stores and specialty chain stores]. However, this dual economy was dominant specially during the years of recovery after World War II. Since 1970, the labor market has become affluent in Japan and the motivation for setting up a small retail store to be employed has lost its meaning over the years. Potjes et. al. (1992) treated this as an important reason for the slow-down of start-ups in Japanese retailing.

Japanese wholesale: a multi-tiered distribution system

The second salient feature of the Japanese distribution system is its multi-layered wholesale sector. Japanese distribution channels are generally longer and involve more participants than their Western equivalents (Fahy & Taguchi, 1995). Wholesale organizations not only are large in number but also tend to exhibit an extremely wide range of sizes. Very large and highly integrated general wholesale organizations co-exist with small organizations engaged in the local distribution of one product only. The large and highly integrated general wholesale organizations are also commonly referred to as general trading companies (*sogo shosha*). The basic functions of *sogo*

7.2 Basic Features of Changes in Distribution Structure

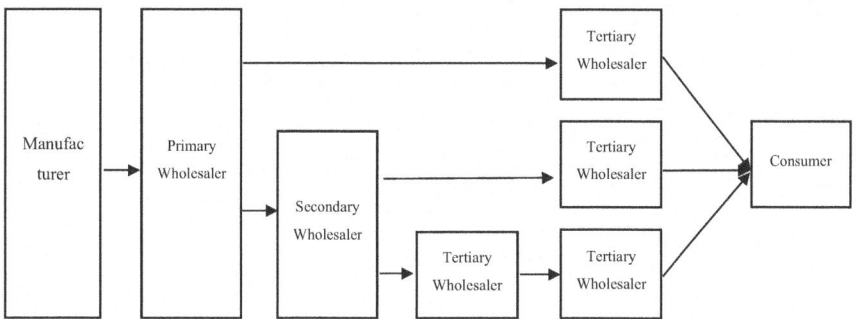

Fig. 7.1 Multi-tiered distribution system of Japanese wholesale. *Source* Based on Ito and Maruyama (1990)

shosha include trade promotion, market consulting, inventory maintenance, freight forwarding, information gathering, and technology acquisition (Dodwell Marketing Consultants, 1985).

Ito and Maruyama (1990) distinguish between primary, secondary and tertiary wholesalers. Primary wholesalers are manufacturer's subsidiaries that deal exclusively with the manufacturer's brand or that deals with brands from various manufacturers. Secondary wholesalers are typically regional distributors. They consolidate a variety of goods purchase from primary wholesalers and distribute the merchandise to medium-sized retail outlets and to a vast network of sub-wholesalers (i.e., tertiary wholesalers). Tertiary wholesalers are typically local distributors. They deliver a wide assortment of goods in small quantities to so-called "mom-and-pop" stores. They also maintain large inventories, makw quick deliveries, accept unsold goods, and send some of their employees to promote special sales for mom-and-pop stores Ito and Maruyama (1990), Fahy and Taguchi (1995). Wholesalers were facing with increasing pressure for changes during the 1990s and they reviewed to channel strategy subsequently. Figure 7.1 shows the traditional multi-tiered distribution system of Japan.

Table 7.1 shows some characteristics of the Japanese distribution system from the end of 1990s to the 2010s. It shows from the table that the number of retail shops in all aspects has been decreased from the mid-1990s to the 2010s. Number of workers employed in retail shops also has been decreased over the same period. On the other hand, the number of wholesale outlets has been increased sharply from 1985 to 1990. The number of wholesale outlets started to decrease in the beginning of 2000s which continue to shrink gradually. Number of persons working in wholesale outlets has been fluctuated slightly from the beginning of the 1990s to the 2010s. Yen appreciation, the bubble economy, and large-scale retail store law in the 1990s are the prime reasons to slump the number of distribution outlets.

Itoh (1991) confirmed another important characteristic of the Japanese distribution market is that goods go through many layers of wholesalers. To confirm the existence of a multilayer structure, one calculates the ratio of the amount of wholesale transactions to the amount of retail transactions (W/R). Itoh (1991) mentioned

Table 7.1 An overview of Japanese distribution market from 1985 to 2016

	1985	1990	1995	2000	2005	2012	2016
Retailers							
Shop Density							
No. of Shops/1000 km^2	4311	4231	3969	3722	3276	2734	2620
No. of Shops/population of 10,000	135	129	119	111	97	81	78
No. of workers per shop	3.9	2.29	2.03	1.75	1.59	1.39	1.29
Wholesalers							
Shop Density							
No. of Shops/1000 km^2	1093	1259	1136	1126	993	983	965
No. of Shops/ population of 10,000	34	38.5	34.1	33.5	29.3	29.1	28.7
No. of workers per shop	9.7	9.97	9.37	9.47	9.8	9.72	9.25

Source Author's Calculation from the data of Ministry of Economy, Trade and Industry, and Ministry of Internal Affairs and Communications

that the higher the ratio is, the more wholesalers are involved in transactions. Table 7.1 shows that multilayer wholesale distribution channel has been shorten due to gradual decrease of retail outlets. Previous studies Flath (1990), Nariu (1994) identified that the ubiquity of retail stores in Japan is often identified as one reason why the number of wholesale steps is multilayered.

7.3 Factors Affecting Changes in the Wholesale Structure

With the advent of mass production of consumer goods in Japan in the 1970s and 1980s, the scale of some producers grew large and they themselves took on tasks that had previously been left to independent wholesalers. The essential impetus for mass production was to achieve scale economies. The following table shows that the number of wholesale outlets decreased gradually over the time. The reason behind this declining scenario of wholesale outlet is to rising consumer product makers which empowered them to gain the market power and began themselves to intensely promote their own brands. Once a brand was established, information gaps between producers and retailers were closed, and little necessity for intermediation by wholesalers remained (Maruyama, 2004). Table 7.2 also shows that the growth of sales per outlets and growth of sales per employee from the 1980s to 2010s has been fluctuated sharply. Because of increasing supermarkets, specialized chain shops and 100-yen shops the growth of sales and growth of employees in Japanese wholesale sector have been increased in 2016 largely. This may have promoted Japanese producers of consumer goods to organize wholesalers and retailers of their wares into distribution Keiretsu, as proposed by Torii and Nariu (2004).

As manufacturers in Japan organized wholesalers into distribution Keiretsu, displacing the wholesalers as channel leaders, they introduced the same sort of liberal

7.3 Factors Affecting Changes in the Wholesale Structure

Table 7.2 An overview of wholesale distribution structure in Japan

Year	Number of establishments	Number of employees (1,000)	Annual sales of goods (billion yen)	Sales per shops (billion yen)	Growth (%)	Sales per employee (billion yen)	Growth (%)
1982	428,858	4,091	398,536	0.93		97.42	
1985	413,016	3,998	427,751	1.04	10	106.99	9
1988	436,421	4,332	446,484	1.02	−1	103.07	−4
1991	475,983	4,773	573,165	1.20	15	120.08	14
1994	429,302	4,581	514,317	1.20	−1	112.27	−7
1997	391,574	4,165	479,813	1.23	2	115.20	3
1999	425,850	4,496	495,453	1.16	−5	110.20	−5
2002	379,549	4,002	413,355	1.09	−7	103.29	−7
2004	375,269	3,804	405,497	1.08	−1	106.60	3
2007	334,799	3,526	413,532	1.24	13	117.28	9
2012	371,663	3,821	365,480	0.98	−26	95.65	−23
2014	382,354	3,932	356,651	0.93	−5	90.70	−5
2016	364,814	3,941	436,522	1.20	22	110.76	18

Source Author's calculation from the data of Ministry of Economy, Trade and Industry

returns policy with the wholesalers that the wholesalers had earlier adopted with respect to retailers, and for the same reason. Recommendations by retailers became important to sales promotion efforts since brands of consumer products became established. Producers began to deal directly with retailers to exhale such efforts and side—stepped wholesalers in some cases. This gave rise to virtuous cycle in which retailers cooperated with manufacturers to plan and develop products that better fit the needs of their customers, which in turn led to stronger recommendations by retailers and still greater scale economies for manufacturers.

The Fig. 7.2 shows that how the growth of wholesale distribution changed over the aforesaid period. In Chap. 4, we discussed that 100-yen shops, specialized home appliance companies, specialized cloth stores, and drug stores are collaborating directly with manufacturers to design the products. None of these changes evicted independent wholesalers completely. This was because the share of large—scale retail stores, that is, chain stores, was small, and independent wholesalers continued to mediate between the producers and the numerous small stores remaining in the market. Therefore, the main challenge for independent wholesales in Japan is extending large—scale retail stores, that is chain stores, across the country. In this situation, it was more advantageous for large—scale retailers to leave distribution to incumbent wholesalers than to construct a whole new logistic system (Larke & Davies, 2007). Thus, the structure of distribution channel did not change abruptly, but changed gradually, as parts of the earlier system persisted.

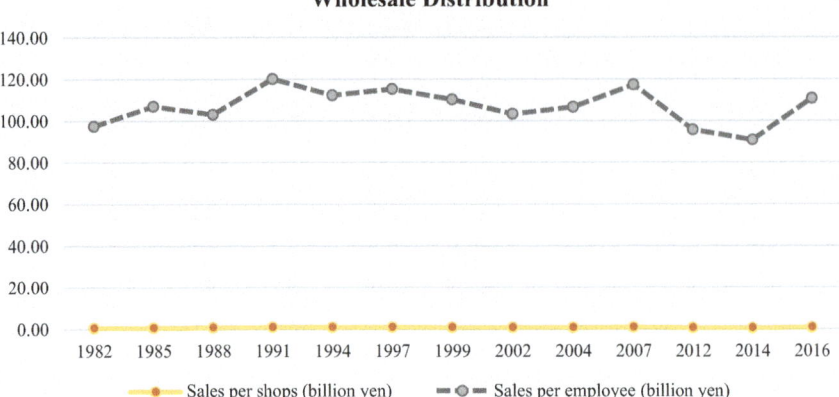

Fig. 7.2 Growth of wholesale distribution. *Source* Author figures out from the data of Ministry of Economy, Trade and Industry

The Table 7.3 shows that Ministry of Economy, Trade and Industry (METI) categorize wholesale industry from 2 or less employees to 100 or more employees in 2007. In contrast, METI extended the category of wholesale industry from 2 or less to 500 or more employees. The structure of wholesale market was extended due to

Table 7.3 An overview of wholesale distribution by type of employees

2007				2013			
Number of employees	Number of shops	Number of employee (1000)	Annual sales (billion Yen)	Number of employees	Number of shops	Number of employee (1000)	Annual sales (billion Yen)
2 or less	77,225	129	6,466	2 or less	72,616	116	8,689,063
3–4	78,447	271	15,643	3–4	61,568	211	14,246,688
5–9	90,750	595	45,721	5–9	67,798	445	38,718,048
10–19	52,075	695	62,742	10–19	38,149	508	50,150,587
20–29	16,273	386	38,466	20–29	12,003	284	31,547,500
30–49	11,286	424	44,992	30–49	8,260	309	34,091,672
50–99	6,069	409	52,100	50–99	4,341	294	42,625,240
100 or more	2,674	617	147,402	100–199	1,480	199	33,659,777
				200–299	347	84	12,597,697
				300–499	229	85	13,480,462
				500 or more	217	234	60,631,050

Source Census of Commerce 2007 and 2913, Ministry of Economy, Trade and Industry

7.3 Factors Affecting Changes in the Wholesale Structure

Table 7.4 An overview of retail distribution by type of employees

2007				2013			
Number of employees	Number of shops	Number of employee (1000)	Annual sales (billion Yen)	Number of employees	Number of shops	Number of employee (1000)	Annual sales (billion Yen)
2 or less	503,844	795	7,251	2 or less	350,996	557	5,537
3–4	252,687	859	11,891	3–4	171,877	583	8,631
5–9	201,818	1,302	24,012	5–9	133,251	859	17,715
10–19	114,397	1,543	27,488	10–19	75,772	1,029	21,466
20–29	32,352	758	12,731	20–29	23,681	557	11,008
30–49	17,229	646	12,122	30–49	13,642	511	10,358
50–99	10,827	738	14,638	50–99	9,160	632	13,122
100 or more	4,705	938	24,573	100 or more	4,483	804	22,650

Source Census of Commerce 2007 and 2913, Ministry of Economic, Trade and Industry

the extension of floor size and expansion of operation of some wholesale categories, like—drinks and beverages, bread, and vegetables. The Table 7.3 depicts that in terms of employee categories, though the number of the wholesale outlets and the number of employees decreased gradually the overall sales increased in the beginning of the 2010s.

Table 7.4 shows, in terms of persons engaged in retail industry, the number of shops, number of employees and annual sales have been dropped sharply from 2007 to 2013. Since the 1990s, advances in technology have enabled the supply of a greater variety of goods than ever before without the sacrifice of scale of economies. As it has become economical for producers to accommodate the diverse preferences of consumers, rapid analyses of demand information have become more valuable in fine product planning (Torii & Nariu, 2004). This is especially crucial for merchandise such as fashion industry where products are highly varied, and consumers' preferences change quite rapidly. For these types of products, direct contact with consumers has become more important as a means of gathering information and influencing fashions. For this reason, some manufacturers of apparel in Japan have now advanced into the retail market. Moreover, as large—scale retailers, that is chain stores, have gained larger shares and their names have become popular among consumers, the information gap between producers and retailers have narrowed recent decades.

The Nihon Keizai Shimbunsha (1999) attributes the decline in sales among secondary wholesalers indicated by the 1997 Census of Commerce to (1) the fact that many of the businesses that sell goods to small and medium-sized retail stores, which have reported declines in performance due to the ongoing recession and increasing competition, are secondary wholesalers, and (2) a growing trend among trading companies, which have conventionally served as secondary wholesalers, toward forming ties with producers to become primary wholesalers.

However, the changes took place in the wholesale structure because of changes in the retail structure that are triggering changes in the wholesale structure, the penetration of information network technologies, such as point-of-sale (POS) data management and electronic data interchange (EDI) systems into the distribution sector, and the effects of new distribution strategies, such as supply chain management (SCM) efforts and other strategic alliances between manufacturers and distributors through efficient consumer response (ECR) or quick response (QR) systems, and also, logistics system reforms initiated by convenience stores.

7.4 Strategic Changes in Distribution Channel

Merger and Alliances

In the 1990s, amid the prolonged recession that followed the collapse of the bubble economy and the continued decline in the number of retail stores, the number of retail stores in the various commodities and automobile industries rose. However, the number of retail stores continued to fall in the food and beverage industry, furnishings, fixtures, and household appliances industry, as well as in the fabrics, apparel, and accessories industry, marking a serious decline in the number of retail stores in all three essential sectors: food, clothing, and shelter. The trends of Japanese distribution system figures by wholesale and retail as reported in the Census of Commerce, "Statistics by Business Classification" (Wholesale and Retail Trade) are useful in identifying the causes of the decline in the number of wholesale and retail outlets in the 2000s and 2010s (see Tables 7.1, 7.2 and 7.3).

Large—scale retail companies are conducting with leading wholesalers. To do business with these retailers, wholesalers have to have a nationwide network. For this reason, the wholesalers rapidly pursued mergers and acquisitions with regional wholesalers, and this promoted significant changes in the intermediate distribution structure. The remarkable changes in mergers and alliances of Japanese distribution industry took place at the end of the 1990s and at the beginning of the 2000s. For example, Paltac, headquartered in Osaka, engaged in repeated mergers with fifteen regional wholesalers starting in the mid-1990s. In 2004, Daika (headquartered in Hokkaido), Itoi (headquartered in Nagoya), Sanbic (headquartered in Fukuoka), and Tokukura (headquartered in Tokushima) merged to form a new company, Arata, a national wholesaler whose coverage extends all over the country except Okinawa. The remarkable mergers in the processed food sector appeared in 2004. Itochu corporation merged with Yuki-jirushi Access, which itself was formed by a merger between five wholesalers affiliated with Snow Brand Milk Products. In 2003, a subsidiary of Ryoshoku, a Mitsubishi Group company, merged with Yukiwa (a refrigerated and frozen foods wholesale subsidiary of Nichirei), with the goal of allowing both to strengthen their low-temperature logistics and to supply products at all temperatures.

Changes in Distribution Channel

Distribution channel for processed foods and everyday goods has been changed at the end of the 1990s. Processed foods include condiments, preserved foods such as canned goods and rehydratable noodles, and refrigerated and frozen foods, while everyday goods include toiletries such as soap and cleansers, cosmetics, and kitchen products such as paper products and plastic wrap. The processed foods and everyday goods distribution channels structure has shifted from "traditional channels" to "new channels." Figure 7.2 illustrates the transformation of distribution system from traditional channels to new ones. Traditional channels are the channels brought about by the rise of supermarkets in the 1960s. General merchandise stores stocked an assortment of products, offering consumers the convenience of one-stop shopping. However, the relationship between the manufacturer and the wholesaler remained organized as before, that is, one in which the wholesaler was a designated agent of the manufacturer.

The "new channels" were initially developed by convenience stores, but later spread to the general merchandise stores as well. They are characterized by the "consolidation of suppliers" and "joint distribution." That is, instead of delivering goods to retail stores using many different trucks of individual manufacturers or products, goods are sent to a joint distribution center designated by the retail company or to a primary warehouse for processing. At these facilities, the products, which had been sorted by category, are re-sorted based on their retail store destination, and then delivered in bulk to each outlet.

In the processed food products sector, vendors are increasingly being narrowed down to only one or a few companies. The everyday goods sector still operates under the designation system (a system in which the retailer's seller is designated by the manufacturer). Given the large number of product items, the trend toward joint distribution is growing. Thus, the responsibility for product assortment is shifting upstream to the wholesale level from the retail level, while the structure of distribution channels is shifting from the conventional structure separated by industry to a new structure separated by retail business type and company.

Under the traditional system, transactions between manufacturers and wholesalers were conducted through "selective channels" whereby wholesalers acted as designated agents for a specific manufacturer. Transactions between wholesalers and retailers, however, were conducted through "open channels" whereby retailers placed orders with multiple wholesalers. Under this structure, the primary functions of the wholesaler were to serve as a sales agent for the manufacturer (product dispersal) and to aggregate demands at the retail level. On the other hand, under the new channel system, transactions between manufacturers and wholesalers are conducted through "open channels" based on transactions with joint distribution centers, primary warehouses, and full line wholesalers. Transactions between wholesalers and retailers, meanwhile, are conducted through bulk order and bulk delivery-oriented "selective channels," a result of the "consolidation of vendors" through primary warehouses, joint distribution centers, and retail company exclusive wholesalers. In this environment, the primary function of the wholesaler is to act as the buying agent for the retailer (product delivery) and to communicate store-specific demand-related information (Fig. 7.3).

Changes in Logistical Systems

In the Japanese retail market, because of the limited availability of store space, the increase in the number of product items has increased retail inventory costs, as retailers have been forced to place high frequency, small-quantity orders for a diverse array of products. Products have been ordered in increasingly smaller units since the 1980s, from the conventional case or dozen to the half-case and even down to two or three individual units of a particular product. As a result, delivery (distribution) frequency has increased from once a week to twice a week, and sometimes daily.

However, high-frequency, small-quantity orders also increase the retailers' expenditures on behind-the-counter tasks such as receiving, inspection, and displaying. Thus, retail companies are promoting logistics system reforms so that products from various vendors are collected at a distribution center or primary warehouse, processed to simplify the work that has to be done in the store, and sorted by store and category for delivery in periodic bulk deliveries. Maruyama (2004) mentioned two cases to understand the transformation of logistical system at the end of the 1990s.

Ito-Yokado's processed food logistics reforms are based on the primary warehouse system (madoguchi donya) established in 1985. Prominent warehouses in each area are designated as primary warehouses. Products stocked at other warehouses are sent to the primary warehouses, which then collect all processed foods regardless of the manufacturer or product, sort it by store, and deliver it directly to Ito-Yokado stores.

By contrast, Daiei's processed food logistics system is based on a system of company-owned regional distribution centers (RDC). The function and role of these RDCs is to achieve efficiency through bulk distribution tied to the store's operations. RDCs strive to improve the efficiency of behind-the-counter operations at retail stores by sorting products by store and sales department and inspecting the products.

Some of the most fundamental factors influencing the channel environment are innovations in information technology and their penetration into the marketplace. IT innovations have a significant impact on both distribution costs and the coordination of decision making within distribution channels and have led to three important shifts in distribution strategies.

Second, as point-of-sale systems come into more widespread use at the retail level, information technology is being deployed in the placement and receiving of orders with vendors. The widespread deployment of POS (Point of Sales) and EDI (Electronic Data Interchange) systems facilitates the sharing of information about individual products, resulting in a shift in production systems from centralized production, which requires economies of scale, to decentralized production, which requires economies of scope. As a result, there has been a shift from distribution channels that accommodate aggregate demand to channels that accommodate individual demand.

Third, there has also been a shift in marketing strategies. Conventional marketing strategies are comprised of three components: (1) the pursuit of economies of scale through forecast-based production, (2) push strategies for selling speculative

7.4 Strategic Changes in Distribution Channel

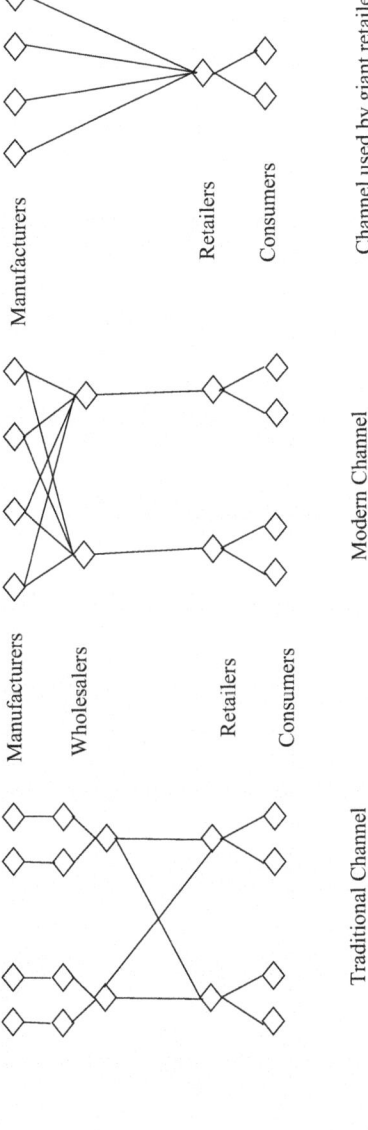

Fig. 7.3 Transfiguring Japanese distribution channel at the end of the 1990s

inventory through proprietary channels, and (3) an emphasis on sharing the risk of overstock through rebates and product returns.

7.5 A New Horizon in the Japanese Distribution System

The Japanese distribution system of the 1990s has been considered as a revolutionary change. This transformation was related to number of factors, most significantly deregulation, stricter application of fair-trade regulations, changes in consumer behavior, entry of foreign retailers and increasing imports through the appreciation of the yen. The most significant and successful change in distribution channels of Japanese retailing ascended after the introduction of convenience store. Meyer-Ohle (2003) described, with convenience store companies having proceeded so far already in the organization of their supply chains, Seven-Eleven finally went even one step further. In November 1997, Seven-Eleven organized 25 wholesalers to establish a separate new company with the exclusive purpose of supplying the company's convenience stores with daily miscellaneous goods and sundries. The establishment of this company was its final move to transform a manufactured-oriented distribution structure into a retail oriented one. Eventually, this newly developed distribution channel (Fig. 7.4) was followed by those retailers which are characterized by small sales floors, limited storage space, broad assortments and long business hours.

However, the retail industry is entering into a period of major transformation. In addition to traditional entities such as department stores, supermarkets and convenience stores, new retail business forms are emerging, including mega shopping mall developments led by real estate companies and JR train terminals being turned into retail centers.

Given that Japan's domestic market will inevitably shrink as the population declines, retail businesses need to generate innovative ideas and services to survive the competition. They must strive to meet the diversifying needs of consumers—ranging from elderly couples to single-member households.

Forty years after the first full-scale convenience store chain was established in Japan, convenience stores are the most familiar retail outlet for many consumers and there are 50,000 nationwide. There is a view that the number of convenience stores has reached its limit given their ubiquitous presence in large cities. But operators of

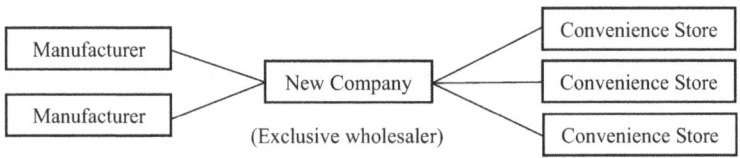

Fig. 7.4 New approach of distribution system by seven-eleven (from March 1998). *Source* Adopted from Meyer-Ohle (2003)

such chains remain aggressive in their expansion. Some of them are pushing tie-ups with companies from other sectors. FamilyMart, for example, is developing business ties with agricultural cooperatives, pharmacies, restaurant chains and karaoke bars in its attempt to open "conglo-retail" shops. Seven-Eleven Japan has allied with West Japan Railway Co. and hopes to place kiosks and convenience stores operating in railway stations in the Hokuriku, Kinki and Chugoku regions under its fold. Seven & i Holdings chairman Toshifumi Suzuki is confident that the number of convenience stores in Tokyo has not yet reached a saturation point. Seven & i Holdings plans to open more stores in rural parts of the country as well.

Supermarket chains, which traditionally feature large-scale stores, are on the defensive in the competition with convenience stores. But now they are starting to increase the number of small-scale shops in city centers.

All retail businesses must strive to increase the level of customer convenience. They need to shorten the time needed for shopping as well as consider offering home delivery of customer purchases, especially in light of the growing ranks of households composed of elderly people.

Younger consumers increasingly rely on Internet portals like Rakuten and Amazon to satisfy their shopping needs. The retail industry must learn how to make traditional stores, which play a key role in local communities, more competitive. The concept of "omni-channel" retailing, which integrates the services of traditional stores and Internet shopping, may offer the industry a new direction. Customers can order products online if they wish and receive them at a variety of locations.

This chapter includes some graphical analyses to show the factors contributing in the changes in of Japanese distribution system. This study is aimed to continue with empirical tests which can validate the findings of this study significantly.

References

Caves, R. E., & Uekusa, M. (1976). *Industrial organization in Japan*. The Brookings Institute.
Dodwell Marketing Consultants. (1985). *Retail distribution in Japan*. Tokyo: Dodwell Marketing Consultants.
Fahy, J., & Taguchi, F. (1995). Reassessing the Japanese distribution system. *Sloan Management Review, 36*(Winter), 49–61.
Flath, D. (1990). Why are there so many retail stores in Japan. *Japan and the World Economy, 2*, 365–386.
Ito, T., & Maruyama, M. (1990). Is the Japanese distribution system really inefficient? National Bureau of Economic Research, Massachusetts, Cambridge, Working Paper No. 3306.
Itoh, M. (1991). *The Japanese distribution system and access to the Japanese market* (pp. 175–190). University of Chicago Press.
Larke, R., & Davies, K. (2007). Recent changes in the Japanese wholesale system and the importance of the *Sogo Shosha. International Review of Retail, Distribution and Consumer Research, 17*(4), 377–390.
Meyer-Ohle, H. (2003). *Innovation and dynamics in Japanese Retailing: From techniques to formats to systems*. Palgrave Macmillan.
Maruyama, M. (2004). Japanese distribution channels: Structure and strategy. *Japanese Economy, 32*(3), 27–48.

Nariu, T. (1994). Ryuutsuu no keizai riron (The economic theory of marketing), Nagoya shuppankai.
Nihon Keizai Shimbunsha. (1999). Ryutsu Keizai no Tebiki (Handbook of Distribution Economy), Tokyo.
Potjes, J. C. A., Carree, M. A., & Thurik, A. R. (1992). Japanese retail stores: Regulation, retailer-client relations and the dual economy. Econometric Institute, Erasmus University Rotterdam, Netherlands, Report 9245/A.
Reischauer, E. O. (1977). *The Japanese today: Change and continuity*. Harvard University Press.
Torii, A., & Nariu, T. (2004). On the length of wholesale marketing Channels in Japan. *Japanese Economy, 32*(3), 5–26.

Chapter 8
Summary and Conclusion

8.1 Summary

There is a dearth of studies on how 100-yen chain shops have emerged in Japan, how they have survived, and how they have been managing a well-equipped supply chain. This study has explored the aforesaid research questions. A booming economy and new amendments to the retail law in the 1990s cultivated a new retail environment in Japan, which called forth a turning point in Japanese retailing. This is how 100-yen chain shops emerged in the mainstream of low-cost retail chains, as an important part of this turning point, transforming, after 1990, from a truck-based pop-up operation into an extensive domestic chain of stores that generated 700 billion yen in sales in 2017. The trending downswing of the economy in the 2000s, along with changes in retail law, led Japan to diversify its retail market, such that consumers shifted from popular department stores to supermarkets and the cheapest retail alternatives. I next summarize the key findings.

8.1.1 Emergence of the 100-Yen Retail Chain in the Development of Retail Industry

Chapter 4 examines how 100-yen retail chain stores emerged and proliferated in Japan's stagnant economy and how they were able to adopt effective supply chains in the face of competition from other types of stores. This chapter reveals that the continuous trend of retail diversity favored the emergence of 100-yen retail chains in Japan. Low-cost outsourcing, bulk ordering, acute integrated POS system, uncluttered distribution channels, the distribution of products through *regional distribution centers* (RDCs) and launching *radio frequency identification* (RFID) e-paper in the inventory management system have equipped the supply chain of 100-yen shops to operate effectively and efficiently. Moreover, this well-equipped supply chain is the pedestal of the whole distribution channel of the 100-yen retail chain, and also the reason for economies of scale in 100-yen retail operations. The analysis shows that sales, net income and profit per sale of top performing 100-yen companies are increasing gradually, due to the continuous development of new products and diversification of the product line, advanced technology-based ordering support system, and expansion of new stores with new themes.

An important concern is how 100-yen shops have been surviving amidst fierce competition. From the 2000s, the four leading operators (Daiso, Seria, Can Do and Watts) of 100-yen retail chains employed various growth strategies to survive in the retail dynamics of Japan. These strategies include adopting multilevel pricing, expanding operations overseas, introducing POS systems, launching new store formats, and introducing online shopping. Although information on industry leader Daiso is limited because the company is unlisted, information about the others is more readily available. Seria led CanDo and Watts in introducing an integrated POS system and opening new types of stores that rapidly intensified growth of business. In addition, online selling, product assortment dynamics, trial and error strategy, learning by doing, and a wide selection of products are the main forces driving the survival of 100-yen retail chains in the stagnated economy of Japan. From the 1990s to the 2010s, retailers in Japan, except for 100-yen stores, changed their price policy to adapt to the economic volatility in Japan. The 100-yen retail shops at first provided products at one price (100 yen + tax 8 yen), but recently, they are providing products for 300 yen or 500 yen as well. The 100-yen shops are gradually adopting this multi-price policy to stay competitive amidst fierce competition.

In addition, 100-yen shops mainly focus on selling attractive household sundries, which are nondurable and lower quality, compared with the same product line from department stores and supermarkets. However, the 100-yen product line doesn't include perishable items, as supermarkets typically carry. Department stores, supermarkets, convenience stores, drug stores, and other retail chains maintain larger product lines than 100-yen retail shops do. Therefore, 100-yen shops can easily concentrate on the few suppliers with whom they engage in direct collaboration for product design and manufacturing. On the other hand, supermarkets and other retailers must maintain relationships with various suppliers, nationally and internationally, to manage gigantic shelves of more diversified product lines. Launching special product lines on different occasions, for example—Valentine's Day, Christmas, New Year's, and Cherry Blossom season. This is also one of the strengths of 100-yen shops that has allowed them to survive amidst severe competition. From this perspective, the product lines of 100-yen shops are almost fixed, so they can maintain inventory of a single product for a long time, compared with other retail formats.

Further, less capital and fewer liabilities, compared with other retail formats, have also intensified the capacity of 100-yen shops to survive in the market. Financial conditions and efficient capital management are also very important concerns, related to staying competitive in the market. The annual reports of top performers show that Seria reduced its wage and labor costs, the cost of merchandise, store occupancy costs, and freight costs, though Seria had less capital than Can Do until 2010.

8.1.2 Determinants of Retail Chain Diversity in Japan

Chapter 5 explores the determinants of retail chain diversity in Japan. This chapter finds that the Large-Scale Retail Store Law, the fall of the economy, and rapid urbanization since the 1990s brought a major change in the retail industry of Japan. On the other side, we found that household costs for transporting and storing goods, as well as the inventory costs of retailers also reflected the structural change of retail density.

Having more stores makes shopping more convenient for households but makes restocking somewhat more costly for the aggregate of stores. The greater restoking costs will be reflected in prices, but consumers are willing to pay these higher prices if the added convenience of next-door shopping is worth it to them. The increasing number of cars can make the shopping trips convenient and cheap even if it is not next-door shopping. Using cars, people can go on less frequent shopping trips in nearby supermarkets, drug stores, convenience stores, and 100-yen stores for their daily necessary goods, which saves time and people's consumption costs. The sizes of houses are increasing across the country, the rate of the aging population is growing, and inhabitants are increasing in urban areas, although the number of total retailers per 1000 inhabitants decreased steeply in the 2010s. The expansion of the sizes of houses helps people to maintain an inventory of household goods for a long time, which also economizes household restocking costs. In addition, store sizes have been increasing since 1995 after the amendments to the Large-Scale Retail Store Law were enacted, ostensibly to permit entry by giant retail store chains from Western countries. This was the first wind of reducing the intensity of small stores in Japan. These socio-economic changes make shopping convenient for people in Japan, and changes in consumer behavior have pushed retailers to introduce new formats of retail business.

The advancement of retail chains the increasing number of cars, and the expansion of the sizes of dwellings makes household shopping more convenient and enables economies of scale effects on household storage space and travel time. High household storage costs and low retailer reorder costs favor the rationality of a distribution system with many small stores (Flath, 1990) which is consistent with this study. We found that the density of small stores shrunk steeply, and the number of retail chains is growing, which reflects on the expansion of household inventory facility and declining retail density per household. The decentralization of distribution systems by supermarkets, drug stores, convenience stores, and 100-yen stores reflect significantly on the economies of restocking and reordering the products of retailers and consumers.

8.1.3 Factors Contributed to Change the Japanese Distribution System

The key findings of Chap. 6 unearth the trend toward the shifting of distribution channels from traditional to new ones in recent years, and a change now recognized as the transformation of the distribution channel structure caused by innovations in IT. This study focuses on the distribution of retail chains which render everyday goods to examine the changes in the vertical market structure seen in the relationships between manufacturers and wholesalers and between wholesalers and retailers from the perspective of the distribution channel environment and strategies.

This study shows that recent changes in the Japanese distribution structure include changes in channel environment, such as product diversification, logistical reforms, IT innovations, increasing number of large-scale stores, conglomeration of retail chains, and changes in socio-economic structure. These factors shorten the steps of distribution channel and transform the distribution channel from a manufacturer-dominant to retailers-dominant distribution system. For these reasons, the number of wholesale outlets and number of employees per wholesale outlet declined in recent decades. On the other hand, the number of large-scale retail chain shops has increased since the end of the 1990s with the expansion of floor size and increased product diversification.

8.1.4 Expansion of Dollar Stores and It's Impact on Small Neighborhood

Dollar stores are rising rapidly and two dominant chains—Dollar general and Dollar Tree, which acquired Family Dollar in 2015—have grown from about 20,000 locations to nearly 30,000 areas. Dollar stores are targeting low-income communities and selling small-box products which makes them popular in poor communities. Offering low price products and selling bulk of non-perishable products help dollar stores to stay competitive and multiplying stores rapidly.

8.2 Implications for Japanese Retailing

The retail structure of Japan has diversified substantially since the 1990s because of multifold changes in the Japanese economy. Significantly, the proliferation of small stores has declined sharply from 14.3 stores per thousand persons in the early 1980s to 8.09 stores per thousand persons in 2017, and the number of chain stores with larger floor space has increased gradually. The Japanese retail industry encountered this structural change because of changes in government regulations Potjes et. al (1992), Matsuura and Motohashi (2005), Takei et. al (2006), suburbanization (Flath,

8.2 Implications for Japanese Retailing

1990). Dawson and Larke (2004) claimed the stagnated economy of Japan was the reason for diversification in Japanese retail industry.

Direct retail sales are gradually being replaced by e-retailing like online shopping, shopping in smartphone, which is termed a *virtual store* in the modern retail industry. This format of retailing uses cutting-edge communication technology to economize the costs and time of consumers. Gradually, new retail formats will emerge, and prevailed formats like department stores, shopping streets, shopping malls will fade away due to the steady change of technology and the socio-economic structure, which can pave the way for investigating retail store density.

Although this study explores the manifold development waves of Japanese retailing, there are some remaining issues which should be discussed in further study.

1. 100-yen retail shops don't provide loyalty cards for customers which may help 100-yen retail shops to slim down the product categories. Further study can explore why 100-yen retail stores doesn't introduce loyalty cards for customers like other retail chain stores.
2. 100-yen retail stores are offering products at 100-yen from the commencement of its journey at the early of the 1990s and still they are providing convenient products to customers at 100-yen except *Daiso*. In this regard, the remaining issue for further study is why 100-yen retail chains don't introduce multifold services for customer such as launching multi-price products (300-yen or 5oo-yen), introducing self-checkout technology for saving customers' time, introducing social commerce,[1] and extending business to grocery, as some have already done—*Dollar Tree*, *Dollar General* or *Amazon Fresh*.
3. Given that Japan's domestic market will inevitably shrink as the population declines, retail businesses need to generate innovative ideas and services to survive the competition. They must strive to meet the diversifying needs of consumers—ranging from elderly couples to single-member households. How can 100-yen retail stores tackle these economic challenges is another unfolded issue for further study.
4. Nowadays, online business is one of the prime sectors in the global retail industry. Amazon, Rakuten, Yahoo Auction, and Mercari are popular online retail portal to Japanese consumers. Also, online delivery for fresh vegetables and household goods are becoming popular with Japanese consumers. These online retail companies don't allow any intermediaries between manufacturers and consumers. To stay competitive with the new phase of retailing, what strategic approach can Japanese retail companies adapt?
5. The business field of Seria Co. Ltd comprises store development, merchandise development, store operation, and distribution system. Seria also has wholesale business like kitchen wares and cosmetics. The present study includes annual data of Seria which not only include the data of 100-yen retail business.

---

[1] Social commerce is a subset of electronic commerce that involves social media, online media that supports social interaction, and user contributions to assist online buying and selling of products and services. More succinctly, social commerce is the use of social network in the context of e-commerce transactions.

Further study based on data of only 100-yen companies may give more explicit understanding about the distinct supply chain structure of 100-yen shops.

6. Consumer experience depends largely on a retailer's location, retailer's category, and advancement of technology. Further study can uncover the strategic issues of retailers' location choice in terms of the category of retailers and advancement of technology.
7. Further study is undeniable to investigate the effect of technological advancement and evolving neoteric consumer behavior.
8. Newer exogenous forces such as COVID-19 will influence how shoppers behave after pandemic, and how shoppers choose channel, choose products and service, and make purchase. Further study can extend to investigate the above issues.

8.3 Implications for Retailing in Bangladesh

Bangladesh economy had a strong growth over the last three decades. Gross domestic product (GDP) increased from $31.6 billion in 1990 to $249.7 billion in 2017 at a cumulative average growth rate of 7.96% per year[2] which is expected to be around $773 billion in 2033.[3] Escalating the size of middle and affluent class (MAC) which is expected to be around 19.3 million in 2020,[4] increasing purchasing power, rising participation of women in economic activities and consumers' behavioral changes towards convenience and quality product, brand loyalty ride to a bright future for modern retailing in Bangladesh. In addition, population growth across the country, increasing urbanization and rising income, particularly the growing middleclass population in the country, have been driving the growth of consumerism in Bangladesh, which is expected to be the 26th largest economy in the world by 2030.[5] Mobile technologies and internet shopping also are the new pattern of retail business in urban areas of Bangladesh.

Table 8.1 shows the value-added ratio of different categories of industry in Bangladesh which is calculated from the Input–Output tables. Retail and wholesale industry are the highest contributor in the total output of Bangladesh followed by real state, mining and quarrying, and education industry. On the other hand, the same industrial sectors are contributing highest value-added ratio in the total output of Japan except mining and quarrying although the amount of value-added ratio of Japanese industries are lower than the value-added ratio of Bangladesh industries.

---

[2] World Bank. 2019. *World Development Indicators database: Country Profile*. [Online]. Available from: https://data.worldbank.org/country/bangladesh.

[3] Cebr. 2018. *World Economic League Table 2019*. [Online]. Available from: https://cebr.com/download/5211/

[4] BCG.2015. *Bangladesh: The Surging Consumer Market Nobody Saw Coming*. [Online]. Available from: https://www.bcg.com/publications/2015/bangladesh-the-surging-consumer-market-nobody-saw-coming.aspx.

[5] The daily Star, May 25, 2020. https://www.thedailystar.net/business/news/modern-retail-growing-15pc-year-1662061.

Because of labor intensity, the value-added ratio of Bangladesh industries in total output is higher whereas capital intensity and intensive use of technology in Japanese industries makes lower ratio of value-added in total output. Therefore, further study on the input structure and final demand structure of Bangladesh may provide a clear understanding of Bangladesh distribution system.

8.4 Future Research

There are few studies of 100-yen retail chains in relation to the density of retail industry in Japan. Previous studies such as Toshiyuki and Kazuyuki (2005) focused on how market dynamics contribute to the productivity of retail industry in Japan, Haskel et. al (2007), investigated retail productivity among three developed countries. There also are some previous studies which focused on the impact of the Large Scale Retail Store Law on Japanese retail industry Katsumi (2014), Grier (2001), Lottoanti (2010) the domestic and international issues of Japanese department stores [Creighton (1991)], and the evolution of Japanese retail industry [Takei et. al (2006)]. This study contributes to our understanding of the structure of low-price retail chain shops such as 100-yen shops, the determinants of retail density in Japan, and the factors contributing to changes in the structure of Japanese distribution system.

This study was confined to socio-economic factors as the determinants of retail density in Japan. Location selection, financing, staffing, product mix, and service mix are also key determinants of retail density in a neighborhood. This research follows the social optimality model (Flath & Nariu, 1996) to investigate the determinants of retail chain density in Japan. We recognize that this implicitly overlooks work in other disciplines, such as location characteristics for retail chain density, price competition, and the urbanization of retail chains. The final caveat concerns the omission of several variables that might influence the number of retail chains and focus on limited samples for examining the effect of the social optimal model after 2000. Further studies can uncover the caveats of this study.

A few research questions might consider exploring the future efforts of unfolding the limitations of this study. For example, why is location choice important for retailers, and how does location analysis strategy facilitate the store performance of global retailers? Another related question concerns potential location characteristics for the internationalization of retailers. Simply said, does a retailer's performance relate to the store location's surrounding competitor density? To investigate these uncovered issues, further research can adopt the central place theory (Christaller, 1933), spatial interaction theory (Reilly, 1929, 1931), and Hotelling's linear city model (1929).

This study also examined the effect of factors changing the structure of distribution system in Japan based on the data from Japan's census of commerce. Further research can be conducted on an empirical analysis of the factors that determine the number of wholesale steps in Japan's retail chain industry using panel data from more than two decades of the census of commerce.

This study is confined within the empirical study of the development of Japanese retail stores in post bubble periods based on the data of Ministry of Economy, Trade and Industry. The Input–Output analysis of value-added trade in future study may provide a clear understanding about economic structure of Bangladesh which can further facilitate to comprehend the competitiveness of the distribution system of Bangladesh.

We currently have somewhat incomplete data on individual firms and there are always data problems in ensuring comparability among industries. As an initial attempt of micro data analysis of Japanese retail industry, this study has contributed to understanding strategic aspects of a single retail industry, struggling to survive in the changing economy of Japan.

Appendix

See Table 8.1.

Table 8.1 Value-added ratio of Bangladesh and Japan ($million)

Industry	2010		2017	
	Bangladesh	Japan	Bangladesh	Japan
Agriculture, Hunting, Forestry, and Fishing	0.73	0.50	0.72	0.51
Mining and Quarrying	0.88	0.20	0.87	0.27
Food, Beverages, and Tobacco	0.26	0.41	0.25	0.40
Textiles and Textile Products	0.28	0.38	0.27	0.39
Leather, Leather Products, and Footwear	0.38	0.31	0.37	0.37
Wood and Products of Wood and Cork	0.41	0.35	0.40	0.37
Pulp, Paper, Paper Products, Printing, and Publishing	0.34	0.40	0.33	0.40
Coke, Refined Petroleum, and Nuclear Fuel	0.21	0.30	0.20	0.33
Chemicals and Chemical Products	0.50	0.26	0.49	0.24
Rubber and Plastics	0.37	0.33	0.37	0.30
Other Nonmetallic Minerals	0.54	0.41	0.54	0.41
Basic Metals and Fabricated Metal	0.20	0.22	0.19	0.24
Machinery, nec	0.36	0.41	0.34	0.40
Electrical and Optical Equipment	0.45	0.34	0.44	0.34
Transport Equipment	0.73	0.27	0.72	0.27
Manufacturing, nec; Recycling	0.44	0.35	0.43	0.34
Electricity, Gas, and Water Supply	0.54	0.42	0.53	0.33

(continued)

Table 8.1 (continued)

Industry	2010		2017	
	Bangladesh	Japan	Bangladesh	Japan
Construction	0.36	0.48	0.35	0.47
Sale, Maintenance, and Repair of Motor Vehicles and Motorcycles; Retail Sale of Fuel	0.84	0.43	0.83	0.45
Wholesale Trade and Commission Trade, Except of Motor Vehicles and Motorcycles	0.82	0.68	0.82	0.71
Retail Trade, Except of Motor Vehicles and Motorcycles; Repair of Household Goods	0.83	0.69	0.83	0.72
Hotels and Restaurants	0.30	0.45	0.29	0.47
Inland Transport	0.71	0.63	0.70	0.66
Water Transport	0.66	0.33	0.66	0.34
Air Transport	0.20	0.50	0.19	0.54
Other Supporting and Auxiliary Transport Activities; Activities of Travel Agencies	0.70	0.55	0.69	0.57
Post and Telecommunications	0.69	0.62	0.68	0.64
Financial Intermediation	0.70	0.63	0.71	0.61
Real Estate Activities	0.92	0.87	0.91	0.86
Renting of M&Eq and Other Business Activities	0.79	0.62	0.77	0.64
Public Administration and Defense; Compulsory Social Security	0.75	0.68	0.74	0.70
Education	0.85	0.83	0.84	0.82
Health and Social Work	0.72	0.60	0.71	0.60
Other Community, Social, and Personal Services	0.87	0.63	0.86	0.66
Total Output	0.34	0.33	0.33	0.33

Source Authors' calculation from Asian Development Bank Multiregional Input–Output Database

References

Christaller, W. (1933). Central *Places in Southern Germany translated* by C. Baskin (1966). Englewood Cliffs, NJ: Prentice-Hall.
Creighton, M. (1991). Maintaining cultural boundaries in retailing: How japanese department stores domesticate "Foreign Things". In: *Modern Asian Studies, 25*(4), 675–709.
Dawson, J., & Larke, R. (2004). Japanese retailing through the 1990s: Retailer performance in a decade of slow growth. *British Journal of Management, 15*, 73–94.
Flath, D. (1990). Why are there so many retail stores in Japan. *Japan and the World Economy, 2*, 365–386.
Flath, D., & Nariu, T. (1996). "Is japan's retail sector truly distinctive?" *Journal of Comparative Economics, 2*, 181–191.
Grier, H. J. (2001). Japan's regulation of large retail stores: political demands versus economic interests. *University of Pennsylvania Journal of International Economic Law, 22*(1), 1–60.
Hotelling, H. (1929). Stability in competition. *Economic Journal, 39*, 41–57.

Katsumi, S. (2014). The effect of large-scale retailers on price level: Evidence from Japanese data for 1977–1992. RIETI Discussion Paper Series, 14-E-013.

Lottoanti, M. S. (2010). The effect of the revised large-scale retail stores law on the Japanese Distribution System. University of Zurich.

Matsuura, T., & Motohashi, K. (2005). *Market dynamics and productivity in Japanese retail industry in the late 1990's*. Research Institute of Economy, Trade and Industry (RIETI), Discussion Paper 05-E-001.

Potjes, J.C.A., Carree M.A., and Thurik, A.R. (1992). Japanese Retail Stores: Regulation, Retailer-Client Relations and the Dual Economy. Econometric Institute, Erasmus University Rotterdam, Netherlands, Report 9245/A.

Reilly, W. J. (1929). *Methods for the study of retail relationships*. University of Texas.

Reilly, W. J. (1931). *The law of retail gravitation*. W.J. Reilly.

Takei, H., Kudo, K., Miyata, T., & Ito, Y. (2006). Adaptive strategies for Japan's retail industry facing a turning point. *Nomura Research Institute, 110*, 1–13.

Toshiyuki, M., & Kazuyuki, M. (2005). Market dynamics and productivity in japanese retail industry in the late 1990's. Research Institute of Economy, Trade and Industry (RIETI), Discussion papers.

Appendix

See Tables A.1 and A.2.

Table A.1 Results of fixed effect regression

	LTR_Stores	LSuper_Mkts	LOther_SMkts	LD_Stores	LC_Stores
Cons	24.79	−2.94	14.50	6.02	18.87
	(3.46)	(4.63)	(10.44)	(10.84)	(4.78)
LDPoP	−0.82**	1.06**	0.23	−61	−0.41
	(0.36)	(0.48)	(1.09)	(1.13)	(0.50)
LS_Stores	−0.05***	−0.00	−0.05	0.02	−0.04
	(0.02)	(0.03)	(0.06)	(0.06)	(0.03)
LS_Houses	−2.26***	0.77	−1.93	0.58	−2.17***
	(0.57)	(0.77)	(1.73)	(1.79)	(0.79)
LCars	−0.84***	−0.17***	−0.24**	−0.02	−0.32***
	(0.04)	(0.05)	(0.11)	(0.11)	(0.05)
R^2	0.94	0.43	0.20	0.01	0.58

Dependent Variable: LTR_Stores, L100_yen shops, LSuper_Mkts, LOther_SMkts, LD_Stores, LC_Stores
*** $p < 0.01$, ** $p < 0.05$, * $p < 0.1$ Parentheses are the standard error of the coefficients

Table A.2 Results of fixed effect regression

	LTR_Stores	LSuper_Mkts	LOther_SMkts	LD_Stores	LC_Stores
Cons	25.35	−2.66	13.07	6.71	19.42
	(3.47)	(4.69)	(10.51)	(10.98)	(4.82)
LDPoP	−0.80**	1.07**	0.18	−0.59	−0.39
	(0.36)	(0.49)	(1.09)	(1.14)	(0.50)
LS_Stores	−0.05***	−0.00	−0.05	0.02	−0.04
	(0.02)	(0.03)	(0.06)	(0.06)	(0.03)
LS_Houses	−2.4***	0.70	−1.55	0.39	−2.32***
	(0.58)	(0.78)	(1.76)	(1.84)	(0.81)

(continued)

Table A.2 (continued)

	LTR_Stores	LSuper_Mkts	LOther_SMkts	LD_Stores	LC_Stores
LCars	−0.81*** (0.04)	−0.16*** (0.05)	−0.30** (0.12)	0.01 (0.12)	−0.30*** (0.05)
LDept_Store	0.02 (0.02)	0.01 (0.03)	−0.06 (0.06)	0.03 (0.06)	0.02 (0.03)
R^2	0.94	0.44	0.21	0.01	0.59

Dependent Variable: LTR_Stores, L100_yen shops, LSuper_Mkts, LOther_SMkts, LD_Stores, LC_Stores

*** $p < 0.01$, ** $p < 0.05$, * $p < 0.1$ Parentheses are the standard error of the coefficients

Bibliography

Clarke, P., Crawford, C., Steele, F., & Vignoles, A. (2010). *The choice between fixed and random effects models: some considerations for educational research*. The Institute for the Study of Labor (IZA), Discussion Paper, 5287.

Flath D. (2004). *The Japanese economy*. Oxford University Press, Second Edition.

Greenhut, M. L., & Ohta, H. (1979). Vertical Integration of successive Oligopolists. *American Economic Review, 69*(1), 137–141.

Guner, N., Ventura, G., & Yi, X. (2006). How costly are restrictions on size? *Japan and the World Economy, 18*(3), 302–320.

Lothia, R., Ikeo, K., & Subramaniam, R. (1999). Changing patterns of channel governance: An example from Japan. *Journal of Retailing, 75*(2), 263–275.

McNair, M. P. (1931). Trends in large-scale retailing. *Harvard Business Review, 10*(1), 30–39.

Mukoyama M. (1996). Towards the establishment of Pure Global, Tokyo, Chikura, Shobo.

Stern, L. W., & Weitz, B. A. (1997). The revolution in distribution: Challenges and opportunities. *Long Range Planning, 30*(6), 823–829.

Bibliography

The manufacturer's authorised representative in the EU is Springer Nature Customer Service Centre GmbH, Europaplatz 3, 69115 Heidelberg, Germany. If you have any concerns regarding our products, please contact ProductSafety@springernature.com

Printed and bound by CPI Group (UK) Ltd, Croydon, CR0 4YY

23/03/2026

02076446-0012